STORYTIME...

WITH UNCLE BUD...

FRIENDS...

AQUAINTANCES...

STRANGERS...

JOHN COATNEY

ILLUSTRATED BY SHERRY BEELER

TRILOGY
A WHOLLY OWNED SUBSIDIARY OF T B N
PROFESSIONAL PUBLISHING MEETS POWERFUL PROMOTION

Trilogy Christian Publishers
A Wholly Owned Subsidiary of Trinity Broadcasting Network
2442 Michelle Drive
Tustin, CA 92780

10 9 8 7 6 5 4 3 2 1
Library of Congress Cataloging-in-Publication Data is available.
ISBN 979-8-89041-216-4
ISBN (ebook) 979-8-89041-217-1

This little book is dedicated to
Denni Rae*
… Who still calls me "Uncle Bud"…

"Not to us, O LORD, not to us but to YOUR Name

be the glory, because of YOUR love

and faithfulness."

Psalms 115:1 (NIV)

*A few months prior to this book being submitted to the publishers, GOD called Denise Renee Kennedy to her Forever Home. 1957-2022

Table Of Contents

INTRODUCTION

Howdy Partner,

Do you like good stories—home spun tales that lift your spirit and make you chuckle?

Then keep turnin' the pages of these important papers and meet my rootin', tootin', cowpoke lovin' friend Uncle Bud. He's the master of "ha-ha's", "hee-hees", and "aha's". A sure-fire storyteller "fer" sure.

Written in the homespun cadence of its author, *Storytime with Uncle Bud* is a collection of short stories worth readin' at lunch time, at the barber shop, the doctor's office, or any ol' time. Stories like *Mickey D's*, *The Rusty Dog*, *Hunn-nee!* and many more that Uncle Bud has told for years. Some of them drawn from personal experience—all of them sent from God.

He's been tellin' these tales since the dawn of whenever—and not to just any ole' crowd. Uncle Bud honed his straight shootin', soul stretchin', spirit blessin', yarn tellin' skills on middle school creatures... I mean children.

That's right, I said middle schoolers. The kids who run everywhere they go like a lost little green ball, break things along the way, make loud entrances, hit somebody when they get there, and look at you with puppy dog eyes as they mumble "whatever" from their light and fluffy brains.

Uncle Bud's stories have withstood the inferno of thousands of adolescents' undivided, divided attentions and he will keep yours as well.

These timeless tales flow from the heart of one of God's choice servants I knew as "Just John". I met John years ago when I was a college kid and he was a youth leader. Little did I know that he would become a mentor to me and thousands of middle school and college students.

In John, the Lord blessed our tribe with a down home Bible scholar, life coach, wise communicator, witty leader, sergeant-at-arms, king of pranks, "a friend who sticks closer than a brother" and best of all, an authentic follower of Christ.

There was no doubt the great love of John's life was Jesus. His keen insights of Christ broke the bread of life into morsels of truth our "young minds of mush" could understand while he lived out the gospel in ways we could imitate. His daily practice of "hanging out in God's shirt pocket" after his "quiet time with the Lord" was infectious. It's a holy habit I continue to cherish.

That's why *Storytime with Uncle Bud* is a blessing. Each story sings of life in harmony with Christ's love for us and others.

I'm glad Uncle Bud finally picked up his pencils and shared his stories. You will be too. I know you'll enjoy 'em. They're better than peanut butter and jelly and more excitin' than a stunt man on a wagon ride.

So, sit a spell. Read a bit. Laugh. Learn. Be inspired. Most of all enjoy. And when you're done, pass them down to family, friends, or neighbors.

With love and admiration,

Pastor Chris Edmonds, bestselling author of *No Surrender: a Father, a Son, and an Extraordinary Act of Heroism That Continues to Live on Today.* Roddieedmonds.com

P.S. Uncle Bud's best story is his life in Christ and his

love for Aunt Helen, his amazing wife. She is everything I've shared about John and more. (Don't tell him I said that.) I can't wait for you to read their story—an epic adventure of love that's changed countless lives through their extraordinary service to Jesus and middle school kids.

I should know—because I'm one of 'em.

Foreword

Reader(s) Beware! and/or forewarned…

This little book differs from the norm…

An English professor's worst nightmare… Unless the prof is on vacation and get'n away from work for a while… Relax'n. Enjoy'n a "change of pace" and (possibly) a breath of fresh air while read'n a book that contains no personal pronouns!

Open'n up this particular book is akin to open' up a can of alphabet soup back in the days when you were a little kid. You never knew exactly what letters of the alphabet were gonna be in your bowl of soup… nor the number of letters you were gonna find. And that was important if you were gonna be spell'n certain words… or a *special* name, maybe? That's why it was more fun eat'n alphabet soup when you had plenty of time to "ponder"…. And if nobody was in a hurry, Mom wasn't gonna fuss 'bout you make'n a mess of your lunch.

- In *this* little bowl of alphabet soup you're gonna find an *A* or two – as in *A*uthor, but don't take that word too seriously….

- There'll be some *C*'s – as in *C*ompiler–which is much more appropriate than *A*uthor…. *C*onfession could be appropriate….

- You'll discover several *E*'s – like *E*ncourage'n you to *E*njoy the *E*asy read'n and the *E*ntertain' contents within this "can of soup"!... Maybe even, *E*mbellish?!

- Plus some *I*'s – as in *I*magination, which is a

prerequisite for reading this book.

- There's lots of *P*'s – such as *P*ersonal *P*erception.... And uhhhh… *P*araphrase.

- *Q* for *Q*uestions 'bout when a so-called *A*uthor *C*onfesses on the front end that some, or much, of the soup's content has been borrowed from other cans.

- And the *R*'s are plentiful – *R*eader *R*eflection, *R*elax, *R*emember?… bunches of *"RE*'s" i.e., *RE*vive, *RE*store, *RE*new, *RE*pent, *RE*joice, *RE*charge.

- Sure don't want to omit the *S*'s! – *S*mile, *S*incere, *S*tories, *S*torytellers, *S*criptures.

So please give yourself permission to relaxxx and enjoyyy those smiles as you read *Storytime*… while reflecting back on similar stories you have experienced with family, FRIENDS, neighbors, schoolmates and teachers, ACQUAINTANCES, and yes, STRANGERS…. Stories, some of which are absolutely hilarious!... Stories, that have served you as valuable object lessons (many un-planned)…. Stories that have helped you develop various life skills that you incorporate daily…. And one cannot neglect the sad and somber stories…. Hopefully, you will enjoy a smile or two as you read along… maybe even discover the book to be informative and useful–like jumper cables when your batteries need *RE*charge'n!...

> *"Blessed are those who have learned to acclaim YOU, who walk in the light of YOUR Presence, O LORD."*
>
> **Psalm 89:15 (NIV)**

Helpful Hints in the Reading of Storytime...

Helpful Hint #1

Obviously, the title of a story can oftentimes provide a good "hint" about the storyline. A few of the tales in *Storytime* (purposely) require a bit of head-scratching in order to better decipher possible contrasting words, thoughts, meanings, and/or hidden messages.... And maybe some indication of a "moral of the story" utterance.

Helpful Hint #2

Our illustrator has skillfully produced (the) delightful illustrations featured in each story, illustrations which compliment *Storytime's* efforts to elicit ample Reader smiles and enjoyment. Expect several illustrations to provide a "head's up!"... or maybe an "assist" in helping you meander through these stories.

Helpful Hint #3

Dictionary Definitions simply means that many stories are introduced "dictorally"... by defining a particular word, words, or short phrase that the Reader will encounter in the story. And should the definitions seem antiquated, please consider the source: "The new best-selling American

Heritage Dictionary–the freshest, most innovative, most used dictionary to be published in this century. Copyright: 1969"

HELPFUL HINT #4

For those Readers who are ponderers, the Reader Reflection, Reader Participation, Reader Heads Up! and Insight "sections" afford you an extra few moments to chew through any unusualness being read and/or contemplated, and encourages your personal thoughts and participation. These "tidbits" are sprinkled throughout these little stories for you to enjoy.... So, "Enjoy!"

HELPFUL HINT #5

This "hint" may be most helpful.... Or at least provide Readers the most insight as to why the author/compiler chose to write these stories in a very casual–though not in a careless nor negligent-style, utilizing a natural Appalachian drawl... "writing like you talk." An explanation of which will be addressed in this little book's first story. So please try to be sure to remember HH #5.

HELPFUL HINT #6

When three... or four of these.... appear, it's to signify either a verbal pause in the storytelling... or a needed Reader pause... as in... "What's going on here?!" You might also want to do a "read aloud" to help with the... uh, uh... more *challenging* parts.

GOOD LUCK!!

1

CONFRONTATION

Genesis 1:27

"...GOD created man in HIS Own image..." (NIV)

Appalachians - The major mountain system of Eastern North America, extending from Quebec to Alabama.

Story Participants:

- 1st Man - The College English Professor
    - middle aged
    - twenty-five years teaching experience
    - a Gentleman's Gentleman in the true sense of the word
    - sincere intent and interest in students learning to be successful
    - lifelong intellectual
    - academician
- 2nd Man - The 33 yr. old college freshman
    - blue collar
    - hard working
    - construction fella
    - former Army paratrooper
    - "common sense" guy
    - zero academics

READER HEADS UP! You will quickly determine that the two men described in this story are total *opposite* personalities. Putting these two together could, and finally did, result in an impromptu Professor/Student "conference confrontation".

Hailing from a few hundred miles north of his (then) present residence in the hills of East Tennessee, the Professor was *perplexed, irritated, exasperated, and perturbed!* The source of his irritation was the inability of *his* "senior" freshman to grasp the finer points pertaining to the development of writing skills.

Long into the discussion, compromise seemed an impossibility *until* the tenured educator determined to experiment on his now reluctant student. The English professor, with a minor in philosophy, was not to be denied. He had hit upon a great idea.... Or possibly a last resort. "Why don't you write like you talk?"

It was at that moment Joe College became somewhat perplexed. "Huh!?" Whereupon the professor hastily and enthusiastically explained the solution to their problem.

"Well, it's really very simple, Joe. Sitting here listening to you talk, it has become apparent to me that you have been blessed with the speech pattern common to the Appalachian people native to this particular geographical area. Joe, you simply need to start writing your papers the very same way you TALK! In other words, *write like you talk."*

Somewhat reluctantly... eventually, the younger man agreed to cooperate with the older man's suggestion. Suffice it to say, the young man worked hard, logging the necessary hours to develop the (minimum) required writing skills required for a passing grade. Definitely much harder than the older man worked in "curving" that C!

INSIGHT: Actually, it has been noted by one who overheard this above-mentioned *Conference*, that the Professor did not say, "blessed with ...", but rather, "afflicted with..." the lazy speech pattern common to Appalachian mountain people. It was also noted that Joe College responded to the educator by stating, "Professor, we do not speak with a 'lazy' speech pattern. We speak with the 'relaxed' speech pattern native to this particular geographical area."

CONFRONTATION CONTINUED...

Incite - To provoke to action.

Incentive - Something inciting to action or effort.

Several years after jott'n down the *Confrontation* story, an old friend of the Jot-ter had occasion to actually *read* the story for the first time–a story he had *heard* decades ago. Upon completion of his read'n of *Confrontation,* the Old Friend emphatically stated to Mr. Jot-ter his disappointment that the story line had completely omitted the storyteller's reason for initiate'n the confrontation in the first place... and the Friend was absolutely correct. So, after four plus decades = an addendum... to detail exactly what did happen to provoke the student's actions toward the professor and how the confrontation unfolded.

The confrontation took place some four–five weeks into the first quarter of freshman English. Seemingly, English 101 requirements were 99% theme-writin'-related... in-class 'n out-of-class... obviously, the out-of-class assignments (7–800 words) requirin' considerably more time, effort, 'n knowledge!

Turns out that in a class of 40+ students, ol' Soldier Boy was not the only student experience'n "technical difficulties" in how to properly connect all the apostrophes, hyperboles, conjunctions, subjunctions, etc... that "...express a contingent or hypothetical action." Shoot! It was at least a little bit of trouble tote'n that pocket thuu–sarry–us dictionary just to make sure the spell'n was right.

It's noteworthy (at least in the opinion of Joe College) to mention that the prof's every-day personality could have never-remotely-been compared to the up-front persona of that (then) favorite T.V. personality, Mr. Rogers; but on the morning being discussed (in this story) Mr. Prof was...

"highly irritated"

"hot under the collar"

"out of sorts"

"toasted!"... Your choice.

The prof readily admitted he was "...really put out..." something 'bout have'n "to grade papers until the wee hours of the morn." (But the prof's whinin' wasn't even a drop in the old proverbial bucket compared to the most gentlest of Uncle Sam's drill instructors or jump masters. Meaning the ex-GI was kinda enjoy'n the change of pace.... Until...

The class soon learned why their educator friend was so "...put out 'n very disgusted..." with this particular group of theme-writers.... "I have been a college English instructor for over 25 years and I know when students are not writing their own papers. In addition to being poor students, several of you are dishonest as well! When I call your names, come forward to receive your un-graded papers. Leave the classroom and on your own time schedule a private appointment with ME–within the next five days, or you will fail this class!"

When the prof finally finished his little *lecture*, that classroom got so quiet you could hear those college kids hold'n their collective breaths.

And then it got worse!...

"Susie Jones–come forward and receive your theme."

And as one would imagine, cute little Susie was near tears–embarrassed beyond embarrassment....

As was: Connie Hill
    Ella Miller
    Joe Smith
    Samantha Black

Sam Beeler... all of the accused!

But wait! There *was* one accused student to escape that tactless scene... Joe College. A fact that only further upset the long-time educator, 'cause ol' Joe was absent that day....

Or was he??

Evidently not!

'Cause when the provoked professor departed the hastily vacated classroom, unbeknownst to the prof, an at least equally provoked student followed his leader down the hallway. As the professor entered his office, he *almost* got the door closed. However, being the perceptive person he was, he immediately surmised the problem: a foot was wedged between the door 'n the doorframe!

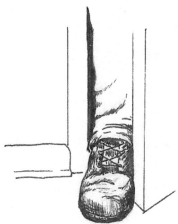

The Confrontation conversation went something like this:

The Provoked Professor's Questions: The Equally Provoked Student's Answers:

"What's the meaning of this!" .... "Sir, I'm Joe College."

"...You were sitting in my class. Why did you not obey

my instructions?"................."Sir, why did you choose to humiliate that group of young people...especially in front of their peers?"

"Just who do you think you are?"................. "I am the man who's going to haul you before the president of this college! And tell him the trick you just pulled... 'n I've got 45 witnesses!"

At this point it's imperative to note that Joe College not one time uttered a single descriptive verb or adverb at his opponent.... (Not that Ole Joe lacked an understanding of such a vocabulary, havin' served three years in his Uncle Sam's military 'n worked on several construction sites.) Also, he was careful to always address the older man as "Sir" throughout the entirety of what turned out to be a rather lengthy, but eventually productive, conversation!... And to be fair to the educator... on two or three occasions at the front end of the confrontation, the ex–soldier had evidently hit the "High Volume" button durin' certain expressed exchanges and was prompted by the Professor to "Please, Mr. Joe, refrain from becoming so loud." And finally, "Please have a seat so we can relax a bit and resolve this issue."

Bottom Line: Issue resolved.... (as was recorded in previous story) Resolved enough for both men to cordially complete the 16-week course on good terms–but never cordial enough to break bread together. And yeah, the professor was sure correct 'bout one thing... Joe College was most definitely afflicted with that speech pattern commonly found among Appalachian folks.

READER REFLECTION: Should you choose to put yourself in the position of either the Professional Educator – or – the Rookie Student (or both men), what would have been your response in those circumstances?... Even more to the point: How have *You* responded in similar situations? Have time and wisdom altered your attitude and responses? It certainly has for the former student and his professor friend. Today, the two men would have enjoyed "break'n bread together" –and the accompanying laughter....

INSIGHT: You, most likely, have already chosen this reference... Matthew 7:12 The Golden Rule... "Do unto others what you would have them do unto you." (NIV)

2

"HUNN – NEE!"

Exodus 3:14-15

"GOD said to Moses, I AM Who I AM…" (NIV)

Honey - A sweet, thick golden fluid produced by bees from the nectar of flowers. A sweet substance or quality. Sweet one, dear.

** The last definition will apply to this story.

"Soldier. Report to the First Sergeant. On the double!" The young private's first thought was... "Uh-oh. Wonder what's wrong?" Upon immediately reporting to his First Sergeant, the Soldier was briefed of an emergency situation from Soldier Boy's home... and was ordered, "Get on the road asap."... The road for this Soldier was a long road.... And especially since he had no personal means of transportation... other than his THUMB....

Soldier Boy's target area was some 400 miles due west. However, several hours later–0200 hours (2 a. m. civilian time)... he was not only less than half way from the designated assignment, he was seemingly stuck in a sparsely inhabited, mountainous terrain on a very lonely, very crooked mountain road. There had been near-zero traffic in either direction for a couple of hours.... In real time, only 10–15 minutes had passed. But it seemed like two hours!

Heck. Just recently his outfit had hit the boonies for a week and had trekked 22 miles in full field gear... on the first day out... and that 30 caliber machine gun weighed 32 pounds... make'n this little stroll down a paved highway a piece of cake. He decided to, "Get the lead out 'n move out! Left-right-left... Left-right-left... Hup-2-3-4... Hup-2-3-4."

Once he got started, only a few minutes had passed when he heard.... Or did he?... maybe he was just hear'n things?... wishful think'n?... Nope–he could hear it for sure now.... He could *really* hear it.... Couldn't yet see any–headlights!... It was a "popeye". Shoot, who cares... Head up–Shoulders back–Stand tall... Here she comes. Thumb out!

She was a real clunker.... What a racket!... And would you believe it?... She clunked and smoked and... rattled right on by... Smoke 'n all. As Soldier Boy watched dejectedly... suddenly the brake lights... Uhhh, a *brake light* flashed; tires screeched very loudly.... It was really quiet 'n dark on that lonely stretch of highway....

Yay! A ride!! That young paratrooper sprinted the 100 yards effortlessly, grabbed Clunker's door handle and jerked open the door of the old car... and was greeted with a rowdy, rousing, robust "Get in h'yar, Hunn – Nee!"

As previously stated, light that particular night was scarce. Even his military train'n 'bout gain'n 'n maintain'n proper night vision wasn't much help.... And to make matters worse, Clunker's dome light was *out - of - order - until - further - notice*.... Only a glimmer of light from the old car's dashboard and the faint glow of several cigarettes flicker'n from the backseat penetrated the dark.... Barely enough light for Soldier Boy to get a brief look at the very friendly lady who was doin' the greet'n.

Before introduce'n Ms. Friendly, it most likely will behoove Readers to visualize a mental picture of Clunker. Clunker was an old Ford. The S/B wasn't sure of the color of the car except to realize it was of a much lighter color than the dark night; an old straight stick/3 on the tree; the identity of Clunker's horsepower was up for grabs.... However, what is important, as relating to this story, the old car was a two-door sedan–a vehicle built to comfortably seat five!

As for Ms. Friendly's boom'n welcome'n "Get in h'yar,

HUNN – NEE", there was a slight difficulty... because there were at least five adults in that back seat... plus three– four toddler/preschool age people. It was get'n crowded in that car. And... as you are 'bout to read, upon climbing into Clunker, things were also fix'n to tighten up considerably for the S/B.

There were only three people in the front seat: the driver... he was not a great big feller, nor was he a small man. Sit'n next to him was a young woman... probably at least of medium build... who was entertain'n a baby, kinda big like, but still nursing on the bottle. And finally, last but definitely not least, ride'n shotgun was Ms. Friendly.... Possibly, her first name was "Very"....

No disrespect, but Ms. Friendly very well could have occupied that seat from shotgun to steer'n wheel all by herself.... And before the S/B could start calculate'n just exactly where he was gonna seat himself, Ms. Friendly kinda lifted him on into Clunker and sat'm right smack-dab in her lap!... just like that baby sit'n in the other lady's lap!...

Soldier Boy's sit'n place had ample width 'n depth, 'cept he was kinda squeezed somewhat towards the dashboard... and height-wise he had to sorta tuck his chin down to his chest a little bit and kinda over to the left towards that *little* baby... who was evidently being fed his "after midnight" meal.

Ms. Friendly must'a been watch'n the lady next to 'er, who had begun bounce'n her baby in her lap, 'cause it wasn't long before Ms. Friendly started bounce'n Soldier Boy on her lap laugh'n 'n joke'n. "Very" got the whole carload of folks in a joyful mood.... So enjoyable that the old Clunker car made it too soon to the turn'n off place where Ms. Friendly's family had to part company with their new friend.

Should one ask that old trooper today if he ever did any hitch–hikin'/thumb'n rides when he was work'n full time for Uncle Sam, he would answer in the affirmative.... And as you have read the above story, you might ascertain that his most *memorable* "ride" was/is the ride down that dark, lonesome mountain road when Ms. Very Friendly opened that car door and shouted, "Get in h'yar, *Hunn – Nee!*"

READER REFLECTION: Have you got a favorite *hitch-hiking* story of your own?

INSIGHT: Oftentimes, opportunities to provide someone "a lift" is as close as next door.... Or right in your own home!

3

THE RUSTY DOG

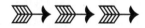

Deuteronomy 31:18

*"The LORD Himself goes before you...
HE will never leave you..." (NIV)*

Pet - An animal kept for amusement or companionship. Especially, cherished...

Though many similar stories have unfolded throughout the years, "Rusty Dog" is one of those worth the telling...

- Early 40's
- Blue-collar neighborhood, low-income families
- Five-year-old boy, 7 years younger than sibling
- A boy growin' up in a neighborhood with few kids his own age and too young for schoolmates.
- An active youngster with far too much energy to be play'n alone.
- Great mom and dad

Recall'n that eventful winter evening when Dad came home with "groceries" stuffed down inside his jacket. "Son, come help your dad get these groceries out of this jacket."

While help'n Dad unbutton the heavy jacket, very much to the boy's extreme delight, out scrambled the *beautifulest* little brown puppy in the whole world!... A night Mom did not mind her supper get'n cold, as the family got acquainted with Puppy.... A second happy occasion for the boy occurred when Mom asked, "What are you gonna' name *your new dog*?" What? The boy gett'n to name his *own* dog–WOW!

READER PARTICIPATION: Think back to your being five years old, and wonder what you would have named a little, fuzzy ball-of-energy that was solid brown from the tip of his nose to the tip of his constantly wagg'n tail.

It sure didn't take the new *owner* of the family's newest member to name "the most *beautifulest* brown puppy in

the world." The owner's new best friend would be called…
"Rusty."

Growin' up in a section of town where most folks'
method of travel was often described as "push'n shoe
leather" presented zero problems for urchin 'n dog.
Inseparable. That would be the best word to describe that
pair. Together, they traversed the various streets, alleys,
short-cuts, wooded areas, vacant lots, and occasionally
trespassed in those (few) yards that were "off-limits".
Those (few) residences where unwanted visitors were
quickly dispersed, "captured", or reprimanded and put on
report to Mom and Dad.

The most offensive trespasses that really upset the
applecart for that pair of neighborhood wanderers were
the unauthorized visits to the little Ma 'n Pa neighborhood
grocery store!

And should Rusty Dog have managed to gain entrance
into the store, corporal punishment for the boy was likely
to be part of the "sentence".

Those months before the boy entered the first grade
seemed to fly by. That puppy dogs were *not allowed* on
school grounds really presented a problem… especially
for Mom. Somehow, Mom managed to keep Rusty Dog
homebound each day until Schoolboy returned home. Why,
folks that didn't know better would of thought the little dog
and the curly-haired boy hadn't seen each other for weeks!

For the next five years Rusty 'n Curly were still
inseparable. The dog, with Dad's guidance, proved to be a
well-trained and well-behaved little fella. Dad had always
referred to Rusty as a "Heinz 57 dog"…. He said they made
the best dogs…. Yep! A really good dog. That little Heinz
57 even learned to "sit 'n stay" outside the little grocery

store. Eventually, he was content to stay with Mom until the urchin returned home from school.

Together, they played "Cowboys 'n Indians" 'n "Army"; hunted birds, "rollybugs" 'n snakes; caught Junebugs 'n honeybees; and played "pick up 'n smear" which was always more fun in the rain 'n snow... especially the snow! Obviously, Curly always did the pick'n up and run'n with the football. Rusty Dog was always responsible for the boy tumble'n to the turf! Simply stated, the twosome experienced all the fun things that kids and their dogs did together.

The boy only had one worry concern'n his little friend. Rusty had somehow picked up a bad habit.... Maybe it was because more people in the neighborhood now owned cars, but whatever the reason, a lot more cars 'n trucks were drive'n through the neighborhood. And Mom said some of'm were drivin' "Way *too fast*!" And Rusty Dog seemed determined to run along beside some of those faster cars... barkin' at them. Dad called it "chasing cars"... said it was important to hurry and "break the dog of that bad habit." Some of the older men in the neighborhood–those men who sat on their porches and in their yards smokin' cigarettes, chewin' Red Man and watchin' everything goin' on... they told the urchin that "old dogs couldn't learn new tricks." Well, what did they know? And besides, Rusty Dog was just five years old, barely half the boy's age, and Curly was only in the 5th grade.

So Curly, Mom'n Dad, and even Granddad, tried everything they knew to *untrain* that little brown dog 'bout car chasin'. Newspapers rolled up long ways to swat that little rascal; tied ' im up = a new experience for that dog; older sister 'n her friends even tried squirt'n Rusty Dog with water/ammonia mix while driving (carefully) down the street. Yet nothing they tried was successful.

Late one winter night Mom, Dad, boy 'n dog were walk'n home from an enjoyable supper/visit with G'Mom 'n G'Dad when Rusty Dog suddenly stopped! Ears stood straight up. Head slightly cocked. What was it that had Rusty's undivided attention? The noise grew louder... and the headlights grew brighter... and larger... and the car seemed to approach faster 'n faster! Zooming by!

BARK!BARK!BARK!BARK!BARK!BARK!BARK! "Rusty! Come hereee!..."

The car never slowed down–only the little brown dog....

For the first time ever, the boy ran faster than the man, barely... While reach'n down to grab the dog, the boy was forcefully grabbed by his dad! The Rusty Dog was about to bite his best friend... something neither boy nor dog could understand....

A neighbor friend brought an old blanket to wrap the injured, frightened dog (to prevent further injury to both animal 'n man). Somehow Dad managed to carry Rusty Dog home and placed him in a corner of the old basement.

Late at night. 1940's. Animal vets few 'n far between. None of which would be open for business. It would have made no difference. No means of transportation... No means of provide'n $$ for the care... that's just how things worked in most blue-collar neighborhoods. Dad did his best to remain positive, assure'n both the boy 'n Mom that, "He doesn't seem to have anything broken. Let'm go to sleep and we'll see how he's doin' in the morning."

To no one's surprise, the curly haired boy was Rusty's first visitor early that next morning. Rusty welcomed his buddy with bright eyes 'n plenty of friendly, doggy licks....

Couldn't seem to be able to wag his tail though.... But Dad seemed to be pleased and Mom was very happy! Off to school. Rain'n, but the boy didn't care. What a long day for that youngster. Couldn't concentrate. Couldn't eat his lunch. A real clock watch'n day... and watch'n the rain....

The 3:00 bell rang and the urchin was the first kid out of the building. The rain failed to hinder the boy from run'n the mile and a half home in record time! Bypass'n Mom's intended hug, he scampered to the basement to see his little brown dog. Rusty Dog could not–and would not–see his curly haired friend again... Ever.... Rusty dog was dead.

The boy gathered the old shovel 'n mattock and carried the tools to *their* favorite hideout behind the old house... returned to the basement... wrapped his little brown dog in the old blanket and carried his burden to the chosen site... and dug the grave.

The rain intensified; the grave was deep enough... Finished... Very gently placing Rusty Dog in his final rest'n place, the boy, refuse'n to shovel dirt on his little buddy, very gently began rake'n dirt into the grave by hand. It was still rain'n when the boy placed an old cinder block and a few old bricks on the Rusty Dog's grave.

The curly haired boy was glad that it was rain'n... or else someone may have thought those raindrops flow'n down his cheeks were teardrops... big boys in blue-collar neighborhoods were not supposed to cry. Not even when his Rusty Dog ....

READER REFLECTION: Seventy years later ol' Curly still retains very fond memories of his Rusty Dog. What's YOUR favorite dog story? What did you say your dog's name was??

INSIGHT: This Boy and his Dog story is a special story.... However, one can never forget Curly's lovin' and care'n Mom 'n Dad who made this story possible!!

4

SALLIE

⫸→ ⫸→ ⫸→

Joshua 24:15

"...me and my household, we will serve the LORD..." (NIV)

Appalachians - The major mountain systems of Eastern North America, extending from Quebec to Alabama.

Hindsight - Perception of events *after* they have occurred.

Sallie was born in October 1891, the youngest of seven stair-stepped young'ns.... One of two gal offspring... a bonny-fied country girl, come into this world only a short haul from Good Springs, which was/is only a few miles from old Hwy. 411 where it runs through Etowah, Tennessee.

Sallie's Mammy 'n Pappy, Amanda Akins-Bivens 'n Abraham B. Bivens, moved from Haywood County, North Carolina to McMinn County, TN in 1871–long before baby Sallie was born.... The reason the family's NC roots is mentioned is 'cause years later their NC background proved to be a *particular* point of contention 'tween Sallie's big brothers and their baby sis.

As the story goes, it seems like anytime any one of – or all of – the brothers wanted to "get a rise" out of Sister Sallie, why, all they had to do was to drop a word or two 'bout the family have'n been run plum outta NC for being "Moonshiners".... They all claimed it was guar'teed to light Sallie's fire!... She had turned out to be just like her mammy, and anything said 'bout the Bivens being "Shiners" opened up the fued'n.

Age wise, Sallie's brothers 'n sister were all pretty much *well-spaced out*, for a 19th century farm family.... Being as in that era, "planned parenthood" was more of a natural and spontain-e-us happenin', rather than any long thought out somethin'.

THE BIVENS SIBLINGS:

1873	John
1876	Callaway
1880	Abe
1882	Easter
1886	Morris
1888	Charlie
1891	Sallie

Enjoy the follow'n and often humorous comments spoken years later 'bout how Sallie's siblings "perceived" their Baby Sis:

- "Ever one of us young'ns was taught to *work*!"
- "… and to work *hard*!"
- "And we all *did*!"
- "The hardest worker of the bunch was our Baby Sis."
- "Sallie could outwork all of us 'cept Pappy."

And as one would expect in a family of nine, a variety of opinions did exist; however, all the Bivens Clan did agree on the family's all-time favorite Sallie Story….

- "Happened when Sallie was close to being eight years old."
- "That be '99."
- "I 'member she was a'help'n Pappy in the cornfield."
- "Yep, yore right… 'zackly when it happened."
- "I heerd some part of it my own self. And I was way on past the creek."
- "Well, all's I got to see was a lil' smoke 'n such."

READER HEADS UP! Count'n Sallie's own generation, this entertain' story has been told to FIVE generations... 'n the most favorite storyteller of'm all is the little girl who actually experienced the... UHHHH event? Spectacle?!

Throughout the many years follow'n *that fearful morn*, Sallie could occasionally be persuaded to "the tell'n of her story"... always an enjoy'n and significant happen' for the whole family. So it was at a 1969 family gather'n, after bunches of "Pleases" and lots of "Purty Pleases", Sallie finally grew tired of'm all a'twist'n her arm, and told EVERYBODY'S most favorite Sallie Story....

After a sorta' slow start, Sallie's tale got to rollin' and she grew very animated with her various facial expressions 'n exaggerated gestures. Her body language was being punctuated with her arms fly'n ever which a'way, all of which helped to paint a vivid picture for all her listeners. As she got warmed up to the tell'n of her story, Sallie's Appalachian twang and pure ol' country "yelps 'n jargon" proved to be absolutely delightful! It was a mighty favorable thing for Sallie's family that their beloved Grannie did not realize that at this time, her story was being recorded! (And is now available on CD.) Favorable, 'cause had she known, it would have been, "No, siree. Not today."

SALLIE THE STORYTELLER

"Now you children ain't never had to work out'n the fields a'pick'n cotton, hoe'n corn, or a'follow'n the mules whil'st they was a'plow'n up all those ol' heavy rocks that we had to carry outta the fields... Phewwwee... Hot!

"Anyways, one morn' late in the springtime, I was

a'help'n my pappy hoe the corn… get'n all them weeds outta the corn field so's the corn crop could grow good…. Pappy always liked to get the hoe'n done 'fore the day got too hot…. Well we'd a'been hoe'n for a right smart while, when ALL OF A SUDDEN!… we heered the most turriblest, awfulest racket you'd ever heerd!!

"In 'em days our few acres of corn was a ways up from the house towards the County Road… NEVER had I ever heered anythin' like it…. Pappy didn't know either what it was that was cause'n all the co-motion… and it kept get'n LOUDER and LOUDER…. Then we see'd all the smoke and such… BIG clouds of it….

"Then… then whatever that thang was, it turned off the County Road and came a'head'n right straight down our wagon road a'head'n towards me and Pappy!!!

"Well… I'm a'tell'n you… I let out with the loudest yell I *ever* yelled…. And I *throwed* my hoe up in the air!… And I started a'runnin' as hard as my legs could carry me…. And I could run fast…. But *that* was the time I runned the fastest of my life–ever!… I was a'run'n towards the house…. 'Bout halfway there I see'd my mammy run out on the front porch…. She'd heerd the racket and was come'n out to see for herself…. Right 'fore I reached the house, I could tell my mammy was unsettled more'n a little, herself…. So, by the time I reached the house close up, Mammy was a'stand'n a'right smart out towards the end of the porch…. And me, still 'fraid to death, I run'd up under my mammy's dress and hid in 'mongst her petticoats."… And right there, Grannie just stopped talk'n….

Finally, one of the younger G'kids couldn't stand the suspense any longer….

"What was that thing that was chase'n you, Grannie?"

"Why, child… It was a car!"… pause…

"It was the very first automobile this young'n had ever see'd."

READER REFLECTION: Your family has stories like Sallie's story. Maybe you or someone in your family has record of some of those great memories?… Sure hope that this story is an encouragement for you to gather up some of the old letters, pictures, post cards, 'n notes; and jot down some of your ancestors stories and 'ISMs for the knowledge 'n enjoyment that can be experienced by both your current and future family tree.

This might be a good spot to introduce ya'll to a few of Sallie's "Apple - at - cha - 'ISMs" which were very much a part of her everyday vocabulary. For an added bonus, enjoy read'n 'bout one of Sallie's lifelong superstitions… one that will surprise you!

Sallie 'ISMS:

- STRUCT'N HER/HIS ONIONS: Used (primarily) on happy occasions and always accompanied by Sallie's amuse'n laughter. Example: When watching one of her G'daughters modelin' a new dress and/or a new pair of shoes. "Look at'er struct'n her onions!"
- AIN'T MUCH PUNKIN': Mean'n he/she ain't feel'n so well or he/she is bein' lazy today.
- GET'N YORE BRITCHES DUSTED!: Pretty much self-explanatory.…
- "QUILE UP!": (quile rhymes with smile) mean'n he/she'd better go and sit down somewhere and be as quiet as a church mouse. "Else ways, you're a'gonna *get yore britches dusted!*"
- THE DON'T CEES: (Curly's favorite Sallie 'ISM) When on a rare occasion his Grannie said, "I've got the *don't cees* today…" the boy knew his special friend was feelin' poorly (at that time) and was need'n to sit a spell.
- SPARK'N/COURT'N: Have'n yore eye on a certain gal or feller.
- SHINDIG: A dance, party, any place where there's lots of folks… a good place for *spark'n*.
- DIS-COM-BOB-U-LA-TED/OUTA SORTS: How a feller feels when the gal he's *spark'n* don't want to do no more *spark'n* with him.
- SI-GOG-LIN: The way a feller walks after have'n too much "shine" after his gal tells him she ain't *sparkin'* with him no more.

- LOLLY GAG'N: Like a'fellar just sit'n 'round not doin' nothin' for lots a days after his gal broke his heart.... He really had the *don't cees*!
- I'VE DONE MY DO!: Finished. I'm through. I quit!

READER REFLECTION: When you have concluded your ponder'n of the various family traditions and/or superstitions handed down to y*our* family by y*our* great grandparents = most likely you are not gonna be surprised when you read about Sallie's mysterious New Year's Day superstition.

Come New Year's Day, Sallie's family always made sure that a "man folk" was to be the first person to enter Sallie's home. Should a "woman folk" of any age be the first person to enter her house on NYD, it would mean bad luck for the entire family for the entire year!

The family's solution to that potential threat'n "curse" was to, obviously, make sure that a "man folk" was Sallie's first visitor of the day. And for several years that *not*-unpleasant *chore* fell upon the shoulders of Sallie's young, curly haired grandson who lived just "spit'n distance" from his beloved Grannie. His reward always included Grannie's biscuits 'n sweet 'tater cobbler pie.... All flavored especially with that not-so-secret ingredient of a grandmother's generous love–which always made those treats so very special!

POSTSCRIPT: Sallie 'n her little curly haired young'n continued their special tradition for several years... until he moved from his Grannie's neighborhood and moved in with his Uncle Sam. Interest'n enough, after livin' with his Uncle Sam for three years, Curly and his Grannie picked right back up on their NYD tradition.... With one slight adjustment... which worked out perfectly, 'cause Sallie always had an abundance of her special ingredient which she also generously shared with Curly's Bride while teach'n her the secrets of bake'n great biscuits 'n such.... However, on New Year's Day, her new G'daughter had to stay outside until Curly had first entered Sallie's home!

INSIGHT: What was the first of the Lord's Ten Commandments that dealt with how to treat other folks?...

5

COOL COUNSELOR

2 Samuel 7:22

*"... O Sovereign LORD, there is no
GOD but YOU..." (NIV)*

Lesson - Something learned....

Story Participants:

• Guidance Counselor - Super heart attitude
  - Age: Late 40's
  - Education Experience: 25 yrs.
  - Head football coach
  - Genuine desire to teach and serve junior high students
• 8th Grade Boy - Rocky
  - An "instant like" fella
  - Who always seemed to stay in trouble...
  - Troubles that eventually took some of the shine off him
• Teacher - Age 33
  - Assistant football coach

Today's Lesson #1:

Morning classes had gone well, and today's planning period allowed enough time to visit with Coach before report'n for cafeteria duty. Most teachers preferred not to act as cafeteria monitor, but the young assistant coach rather enjoyed it... gave him extra time to meet students not in his classes.

Step'n into the office, the secretary's greeting was brief. (she was speak'n on the telephone) "Coach is expect'n you... Said to have a seat in his office... One of the teachers needed assistance... He'll be right back."

Settle'n into a chair facing the large windows look'n

out over the front of the sprawling school campus, Mr. Assistant Coach was just about to get comfortable when Coach ushered Rocky Boy into his office!

Coach simply pointed to the chair where he intended for his loud, complaining young friend to sit down. Sit he did, but the complaints seemed to intensify. The man's finger-to-the-lips "SHHHH" sound only partially shushed the youngster; however, the sudden hard look 'n body language conveyed by the seasoned educator sufficed. It was not Rocky's first time in *that particular* office. And give him credit, one thing the boy *had* learned: enough was enough when Coach was presiding.

As far as his classroom transgression was concerned, Rocky Boy readily acknowledged being *guilty as charged*. But the "unfair" source of his frustration and anger was, "Why me? Why me… when half a dozen other kids were doin' the very same thing?!" Rocky's anger resurfaced and while the boy was venting his frustration, Coach was stand'n with his back turned to the silent Mr. Assistant and the flustered boy, calmly look'n out the window.

(Coach) "Rocky, please come over here a minute."
Surprisingly, the boy responded as requested.

(Coach) "Will you count those cars for me?"

(Rocky) "One, two, three, four, five."

(Coach) "How many of those cars are moving right now?"

(Rocky) "Four."

(Coach) "Which car is not moving?"

(Rocky) "The police car that most always sits in front of the school."

(Coach) "Rocky, if that blue car was speeding... and that red car ran past that stop sign without stop'n... and that white van was tossing McDonald's paper bags 'n Coke cups out of the windows... and that black pick-up truck ran over that mailbox and just kept right on goin'... and *you* were the police officer–which one of those drivers would *you* stop and issue a traffic ticket?"

Rocky Boy pondered a minute try'n to decide which of those cars *he* would stop, when "the light came on"! Or more correctly, the *lights* came on... for the 8th grader *and* the 8th grade teacher! And Coach...? Did he *ad-lib* that object lesson or had he used it before? Either/or, it was a great lesson for that day.

TODAY'S LESSON #2:

Unfortunately, Rocky's story for that particular day was to be continued....

Rocky reluctantly accepted the fact that he was not "being picked on" by the teachers and he was satisfied, if not content, with the object lesson for the day.... Especially when Coach decided the best way to handle the problem was to let the boy off the hook.... Rocky even told Coach that he was gonna play on the football team.

Because Rocky had "been in the office" three times in less than one month, school board protocol dictated that his parents had to be formally contacted, updated, and encouraged to shore up things on the home front. Coach was to notify the parents via telephone of the current situation, with the student present. Mr. Assistant Coach also was to remain present while the call took place... as a safeguard in case of any perceived miscommunication....

And follow'n is the conversation that ensued:

(Coach) "Hello, Mrs. Rocky's Mom? This is the guidance counselor at Blank Junior High School. I was call'n to talk to you about Rocky."

(Mom) "Well, yeah... thanks for calling, but Rocky wasn't feel'n well today and we kept him at home."

(Coach) "Uhhh... did you say Rocky was sick?"

(Mom) "Yeah. Rocky's home sick today."

(Coach) "Well, is he *still* at home?"

(Mom) "What do you mean is he still at home? I'm stand'n here look'n at him lay'n in the bed right now!"

(Coach) "Uhhh... well Mrs. Rocky's Mom, I'll get back to you on this later. Thank you."

Rocky *never* did try out for the football team....

READER REFLECTION: WOW! What are you think'n right now?! Caring folks can help children in many, many ways. But it's not too often that others can do much to change a child's home environment.

INSIGHT: Sure glad there's still folks 'round like the *Cool Counselor* who are willing to travel that/those extra mile(s)....

6

DOC AND THE 'LIL BUCKAROO

Job 5:9

"HE performs wonders that cannot be fathomed, miracles that cannot be counted." (NIV)

Influence - A power indirectly or intangibly affecting a person or course of events.

Story Participants:

- The Doctor - mid 50's
    - an "ALL – Pro" pediatrician for 29 years 'n count'n
    - genuine "champion" of and for children
    - valued counselor 'n encourager of moms 'n dads
    - hobby and method of relaxation was craft'n leather products
- The Family - Mom 'n Dad
    - Baby Sister… age 3
- The Little Buckaroo - almost five years old
    - also one of Doc's regular patients

The two scheduled appointments mentioned in this story were made for Baby Sis…. Lil Buck was just visit'n on both occasions.

Accord'n to his mom, the Little Buckaroo–rather than being opposed to "goin' to the Doctor"–always seemed to get excited for any opportunity to visit his doctor friend. As prefaced earlier, Little Buck's doctor was not only an elite pediatrician, Dr. Rick was 100% *kid friendly*!... with a *kid friendly* office atmosphere, that if not a *one of a kind* then for sure, one of a very few. And this is where Doc's hobby comes into play…. Literally play!... Pun most definitely intended.

READER PARTICIPATION: You are probably gonna need a little extra time on a few paragraphs–the grade is F for sentence structure, etc. and… F for Fun.

Kids soon discovered that walk'n into Dr. Rick's reception/waiting room was akin to being in the local supermarket and leave'n the aisle that displays cosmetics, cleanin' fluids, 'n various laxative products directed towards the old people–and well it was like walk'n toward the next aisle; round'n the corner; and find'n the toys, candy, and some really cool kid stuff.…

The only semblance to the typical doctor's office was chairs for sit'n and the receptionist area for sign'n in… even that was somewhat different. Upon enter'n Dr. Rick's office, unless the kids were really feel'n bad, they didn't even give the chairs consideration. They immediately headed for the array of various leather "goodies" on display: belts of different sizes, shapes, 'n colors; wrist bands (for put'n your name on) of various designs with all kinds of options like butterflies, flowers, horses, and longhorn steer; necklaces; small pocketbooks; toy holsters–"Holsters?!"

Holsters?… for cowboys?… like John Wayne?… WOW! Cowboy stuff was important fun stuff for this particular Little Buckaroo. The reason being–and this source of information comes from reliable (family) sources–Lil Buck's penchant towards cowboys was derived from his dad's affinity for spend'n some of his "own down time" in the TV room watch'n old John Wayne westerns.… And as you… grinnin'… have already surmised, *the Little Buckaroo* is Dad's most favorite "cowboy" watch'n pardner 'n little buddy!… All of which lends credence to the special friendship between Little Buck and Dr. Rick– Holsters! Holsters made especially for both little cowboys 'n little cowgals.

The good doctor, have'n four children and nine G'kids of his own, had crafted more than his fair share of toy holsters.... Which is, in part, how the very "kid friendly" doctor's office came to be a focal point of this very fun... and precious... kid story.

A few days after Thanksgiving weekend Mom's sixth sense detected "something different" in Baby Sister's mannerisms that necessitated an unscheduled visit to see the doctor. And, as always, Lil Buck was excited about the opportunity to see Dr. Rick... annnd possibly... any new holsters that might be on display.

The young Buckeroo was not disappointed. Several new items were there for the children to play with and view.... And there was *one special holster* that immediately caught Lil Buck's eye.... A big black two holster set with toy pistols... big silver conchos with white leather "strings" hang'n down... and red, wooden bullets... with a great big silver buckle.... Bucky could hardly wait to see the doctor!

That day the boy's first, and also his part'n, words to his doctor friend were, "Don't sell that black holster. I'll be back after CHRISTmas with my CHRISTmas money." Unknown to the boy, Baby Sis was to return to the office for a follow–up appointment: Friday, Dec. 27.

Follow'n is Mom's explanation of their December 27th appointment: Caught in unexpected traffic, Mom was runn'n a bit late for Sis' appointment and know'n she would have to find a park'n space, remove the Baby from her car seat and make their way to the office, she dropped the Buckaroo off in front of the office with instructions to "Go to the reception desk and tell the 'lady at the front desk' that Mom is on her way." Wellll, that was not exactly what happened....

Turns out that the "lady at the front desk" was surprised,

to say the least, when the top of a child's head–and then a small hand literally appeared... and *slapped!* down on her desk. A child's voice said, "Here's my CHRISTmas money. I want my holster!"

"The lady at the front desk" had been on Dr. Rick's staff for several years and had experienced innumerable spontaneous moments with children; but this occasion, "Stumped me."And that single dollar bill now lay'n on top of her desk only added to her dilemma....

Gain'n her composure, "TLATFD" picked up that dollar bill... interrupted the doctor... handed him the dollar... briefly explained (as best she could)... told Dr. Rick she was take'n early lunch and on her way out she would tell his little customer that "The doctor will be with you in a few minutes, Bucky."

Turns out that Doc 'n his little buddy had only one minor adjustment to make.... Being as Little Bucky's "purchase" was a bit too large for the young cowboy, he just naturally assumed that the good doctor could make it fit... and "Doctor Rick, can you put my name on it?" Sure he could.... Why, Doctor Rick could do almost anything... except... contain his own delight at his young friend's excitement 'n enthusiasm. Also, the doctor marveled at the Little Buckaroo's business expertise. Who says that a dollar won't buy anything these days?!

READER REFLECTION and INSIGHT: It has been stated that very large treasures often come in small packages... which brings the follow'n story to mind....

Picture please, in your mind, Smalltown, U.S.A.... mid 1970's. It's Saturday and Mom had left home early a.m. to visit *her* mom... leaving five-year-old Joey 'n his dad in charge... of everything!

And you may have already guessed, correctly, that the first order of business the "men of the house" had planned was no business at all. It was simply, sleep in. Which came off as planned. Perfectly.

Breakfast was next. A rather late breakfast. And as far as the boy was concerned, Dad was a great cook. Two of Joey's favorite Pop-Tarts. And it was the very first time the boy had ever enjoyed chocolate milk on his Frosty Crunch cereal. Breakfast was greatttt!

Soon, things got kinda quiet and Dad noticed that his son, like most little folks, eventually started... kinda play'n 'round with his cereal... and soon drifted off into that far-away land of boyhood imaginations 'n wonder.

Finally, Joey started hummin' (a tune unfamiliar

to Dad), so the Head Cook settled back in his chair and listened to his little best buddy. Then Joey began his song:

"The doggie says Bow Wow... Bow Wow... Bow Wow."

"The kitty says Meow... Meow... Meow."

Then came an extended pause from the child... and a rather abrupt change as he sang, "And the flowers talked to me."

And he was through. Done. End of song. And again began tinker'n 'round with his cereal. The room remained quiet for a few minutes until, very softly, Dad broke the silence, "Joey, what did the flowers say to you?"

Not look'n up from the cereal bowl, little Joey softly sang, "JESUS loves me, this I know, for the Bible tells me so"...!

"FROM the lips of a little child..."

7

TOOTIE

≫→ ≫→ ≫→

Psalms 5:11

"...let all who take refuge in YOU be glad..." (NIV)

Admiration - To regard with wonder and approval. To ESTEEM; respect.

Appreciation - Gratefulness; gratitude.

Manage - To direct, control or handle. To administer or regulate. To arrange.

His surname was Sharpe, with an E. His given name was Clarence, with two EE's. In his white-collar business world he was known as Mr. Sharpe. His wife called him Clarence, and his sons knew him as Dad. To dozens of 10–12-year-old boys who played on his baseball teams, he was distinctively 'n affectionately known as "Tootie".

Somehow, that very special man managed to manage Little League baseball teams–for several consecutive summers! Teams made up of pre-teen boys! Boys of all shapes 'n sizes. Boys full of abundant energy... 75% of'm with short attention spans... 15% of'm undisciplined. 100% of'm (in varying degrees) subject to boyhood mischief. As for baseball aptitude, 50% of'm had a difficult time playing roller bat; initially lacked the basic skills to play the game; and as for the rules of baseball... they figured it was okay to just make up a few as they went along. "Oh yeah. What was an umpire?"

Imagine a completely sane man volunter'n to oversee, coach, and teach a bunch like that? How to begin? Tootie began with friendship. That was the very first thing Tootie's boys learned = Coach Tootie was their friend. An adult friend who treated boys equally. Be it the 12-year-old star pitcher or the 10-year-old rookie who hadn't yet learned the outfield from the infield.

Haul - To provide transportation.

Trailer - A large transport vehicle hauled by a truck or tractor.

By the late 1940's, Little League baseball was beginning to gain a foothold in America. In Tootie Sharpe's hometown (pop. 150,000) there were only three LL ballparks, scattered throughout a large geographical area of the county. His boys walked one to three miles to the practice field twice a week. Then another two days per week on *game days*, usually around 3p.m., Tootie would meet his boys to–literally–haul them all to the ballpark... some 8 miles from the practice field.

Fortunately, it was an era when most parents appreciated people like "Mr. Sharpe", who spent their personal time, energy, and $$ to lend a hand that allowed children opportunities to participate in activities that would have otherwise been unavailable to children living in blue-collar neighborhoods. So what if their boys were ride'n across town in an open-bed-trailer with *new tires, sturdy sideboards, 'n locking tailgate....* And of course, all the boys were having a blast! Certainly, it was in the day before seat belts. And if car seats for kids had then been deemed necessary by law, that would've caused a bit of embarrassment for a few of the smaller Little Leaguers– many of whom were the better ball players.

Exactly how did Mr. Tootie Sharpe manage to acquire uniforms / balls / bats / catcher's equipment / and even mange to *annually* arrange a bonafide, Uptown banquet for his boys??... And don't forget the needed transportation for 15 boys!!! All this 'n much, much more is the amazing legacy of an amazing friend.

So what???

Many of those boys who had the privilege of play'n on one of Tootie's teams, when pausing to recall "the good ol' days", can honestly say that, "No boys could have ever had a better friend than Tootie Sharpe!"... And if that boy could concentrate 'n listen real intently... and visualize stand'n in the batter's box when Tootle was coach'n 3rd base, the boy can sometimes still hear his coach say'n,

"You're better than he are. Hit that ball!"

READER REFLECTION: Hopefully, grow'n up, YOU had an adult friend like Tootie Sharpe. Should he or she still be alive = sure bet that a call or card from YOU would make (multiple choice): Their day!

Their week!!

Their month!!!

INSIGHT: Speaking of friendship... Mark 12:30-31! (NIV)

8

SHOES...

⫸→ ⫸→ ⫸→

Psalms 1:6

New Living Testament

Underprivileged - Socially or economically deprived.

Gift - Something given. A present. The act of giving.

Story Participants:

- 11 middle school boys - Residence: Public housing, the inner, inner city
- The Young Fella - early 20's
- The Older Fella - early 40's
- The Givers

It was a couple of weeks before CHRISTmas… only a few more days until it would be *legal* to be out of school for that long-anticipated two weeks of freedom from enforced academic requirements. Maybe it was just a *guy* thing? Who knows for sure? But it was the current, most looked forward to and most discussed topic among many of the boys who attended City Middle School–a school located in the heart of the inner city.

"Boys" are mentioned because when the Older Fella received what turned out to be a very special phone call several days before December 25th, the caller simply and briefly stated, "I have put a check in the mail. It should be there by tomorrow. I am aware of that group of boys you and the Young Fella have been spending time with… aware of their social environment. And I want to ask you to do me a favor."

"Sure!" was Mr. Older Fella's response, the kind of simple, affirming response expected when two old friends conversed.

SHOES ...

READER HEADS UP! Mr. Caller was a generous giver of gifts to others. And equally *very practical* in his giving. Always having pondered deeply how to provide appropriate, effective gifts, while also touching a maximum number of people. Yet, a different approach in his giving seemed to indicate *fewer* folks would be receiving gifts this particular year.

Mr. Caller's initial request of his old buddy to "assist" Santa came as no surprise whatsoever. Nor was his second request about "...keeping the 'source' of this project between the two of us..." unexpected. Surprisingly, request number three *was* unusual. Unusual because, as previously stated, this year's CHRISTmas gift (of $500) was only going to touch three-four young fellows. "I want to ask you to make sure that three or four of those boys from City Middle School get new shoes for CHRISTmas. I want them to go back to that school wearing a new pair of those *Air Jordan/NBA basketball shoes."

*NOTE: In the mid 1980's, when *those* shoes were first marketed, the cost per pair exceeded $100! So, with that initial phone call things looked like Santa was goin' to be especially kind to three–four young fellas. However, as this story unfolds, one eventually perceives that Mr. Caller had just gotten the "basketball" rolling!

The next teammate to "pick up the ball" was a gentleman with close ties to a well-established chicken sandwich franchise. Mr. Chicken Sandwich immediately lofted a near perfect alley-oop pass to another teammate who was in excellent position to complete a slam dunk! It was an emphatic 360! A textbook dunk! Performed by the owner of a chain of... wanta' guess?... shoe stores. Sports/athletic shoe stores! One of which was located in a very large and highly successful shopping mall, 10 minutes from the City Middle School campus. Welcome to the team, Mr. Shoe Store Owner/Giver #3. This CHRISTmas story appears to be head'n towards a win for the home team.

Mr. Shoe Store Owner had learned from Mr. Chicken Sandwich of the initial $500 gift designated for the boys' CHRISTmas surprise. And upon learn'n there were 10–12 young fellows who generally were considered to be part of the group, he was curious as to how it was gonna be determined which of them would be selected to receive the new shoes? A concern to which the Old Fella 'n the Young Fella had given serious consideration.... But only short time consideration, because MSSO was feelin' the holiday spirit. Big time! He simply *eliminated* all problems. "Fellows, you bring up to 12 guys to the store Saturday morning. Each one can select any pair of shoes in the store. (Hold on to your hat, Reader!) The $500 will cover the cost–tax included."

Yay! Yay! Yay! High fives all 'round!

Sure enough, that *designated* Saturday morn', eleven boys showed up at the pick-up point *on time*... most of them did not even notice the rain. After a quick biscuit breakfast, it was on to the mall. MSSO had encouraged them to "Come early in order to beat the crowd." And as you would expect, each young man was more than super excited 'bout get'n their new pair of shoes. Little did they know what *kind of shoes* they were gonna take home with'm. It would have probably been somewhat "dangerous" had they known exactly what was in store for them!

Oftentimes, youngsters have to be "coached up" a bit before goin' various places–the "do's 'n don't's" emphatically presented. It would take far too much space here to describe even their eyes, when told they would *personally* own the shoes of their choice when they walked out of that mall.

There is, however, space enough to mention that the boys did great! Their behavior was top of the mountain manners. Zero complaints… by them or against them. Zero problems… except for a minor adjustment. The store manager did approach the Older Fella to suggest an additional way to accommodate the boys. Seems as though his staff was experience'n an unusual odor in the store that mornin'… something 'bout socks. Half of them weren't wear'n any, and those who were… Umm, Uh, Umm… a fact that may have attributed to the difference in the atmosphere that particular morn'. Turns out the good manager was more than happy to furnish each young man with a *new* pair of socks!

SHOES Conclusion…

In wrap'n up the events of those boys' fun and memorable mall outing that special holiday season, one additional occurrence needs to be RE-addressed… have'n to do with the original giver's, Mr. Caller's, third wish– "I want those young men to go back to school wearing their new shoes… I wish I could be there to see them."

Reader Friend, it is of *considerable importance* to the conclusion of this Shoe Story to mention Mr. Caller's wish was more than adequately conveyed to those boys— collectively and individually on more than one occasion— before they were dropped off at their respective homes that Saturday afternoon.

And surely it's not too late in this story to state that on the day prior to Saturday's shoe day, it had rained

ALL day... 'n ALL night.... And as previously noted, the precipitation was still fall'n on pick-up morning.

Next day, Sunday afternoon, the rain was *still* fall'n when the Older Fella 'n Mrs. Older Fella were drive'n by the neighborhood playground. And might you want to guess who they saw play'n football?... tackle football! In a muddy quagmire!! Five boys on one team and six boys on the opposin' team. They were easy to spot. They were ALL wear'n new, white??... shoes.

READER REFLECTION: If you are a Lady Reader (ASSUME'N you just finished read'n 'bout those unrecognizable new shoes), there's a good chance your initial thought(s) were "Oh, no!"... if you are a Gentleman Reader, then you're wonder'n what position you would have been play'n that day!

INSIGHT: Definition of a servant: "after washing their feet... since I the LORD have washed your feet, you ought to wash each other's feet. I have given you an example..." John 13:12-15 (NLT)

9

"HUH?"

Psalms 25:14

"Friendship with the LORD is reserved for those who fear HIM. With them HE shares the secrets of HIS covenant." (NLT)

Under-privileged - Socially or economically deprived.

Contribute - To bring together, unite.

Story Participants:

- 14 very polite middle school Young Ladies - Address: Inner, inner city public housing
- 13 cooperative middle school Young Men - Address: Inner, inner city public housing
- The Young Fella - early 20's
- The Young Fella's Girlfriend - Early 20's
- The Older Fella - early 40's
- Mrs. Older Fella - early 40's
- Gifter #1: An adult who had grown up in that same inner, inner city public housing neighborhood (as mentioned above).
- Gifter #2: Mr. Dad
- Restaurant Staff

READER HEADS UP! The basis of this little story, *"HUH?"*, is the Twin Sister of *Shoes*… The intros are an echo, with the addition of the girls' participation. However, the message of the two stories makes the tell'n worthwhile. Besides, isn't that the nature of an echo, echo, echo, echo….

It was early spring, seemingly only a few short weeks after the now infamous "Mud Bowl" football game that featured those two teams square'n off in that rough 'n tumble match-up. Remember? The game that was "highlighted" by the participants brand spankin' new Air

Jordans. *See: *Shoes*…

The same youth organization. The same office. The same telephone… Ring. Ring. That same Older Fella answered. The Gifter was different, as was the request. Two hundred dollars were available to take several of those inner city kids–girls 'n boys–to an "uptown" restaurant for a nice sit down meal. "Want'm to get cleaned up and dressed up (as best as possible). Easter is in three weeks. This year the kids are out of school the week of Easter. Sure would like it to happen that week."

Before that conversation was completed, the name of potential Gifter #2 had already entered Older Fella's mind. It was an easy call to make. (Potential) Gifter #2's only daughter had previously been a very active member of the above-mentioned youth organization. Also, Gifter #2/"Mr. Dad", had always continued to "lend a hand" when an extra adult was needed on hike'n trips, rafting trips, and various outings.

Oh… It's probably not gonna come as a great surprise to Readers of this tale that Mr. Dad was the owner of 1… 2… 3 popular steak house restaurants–one of which was located in the general neighborhood in which lived those middle school age PEOPLE who make this story. Hmmm…

Once contacted, Mr. Dad got excited 'bout host'n a group of those young PEOPLE. His generous response was, "Sure! No problem. Just have those folks here 'n in line before five o'clock. That will get them in before the crowd gets here." Also, Mr. Older Fella's question, "There's $200.00, Mr. Dad. How many kids can…" was a question that was never completed.

As already stated, Mr. Dad was a generous person. "Bring a bus load. There's 17 different steak dinners offered.

Those youngsters can choose any item except #17." (Not because of the price of the steak, but because of the extra prep time involved.) "Call me around 10:00 that morning, just to check in. We'll talk then. Thanks for calling me."

Well, folks, everything that needed to happen during those next 2½ weeks fell right into place. When the day finally arrived, 27 clean cut, good look'n girls 'n boys met at City Middle School. Thursday afternoon... 4:00 p.m. sharp... anticipation was obvious... excitement shone in every child's face... the ol' bus was loaded in record time.... "Uunnn, Uunnn"... They were on their way.

While enroute the necessary do's 'n don't's were thoroughly "rehearsed" and the youngsters were "reminded" of the proper method of how to politely order their meal. All i's dotted and t's crossed.... Really?? Forty-five minutes later those 27 Happy Campers, along with their four adult buddies, quietly filed into that BIG fine-look'n steak house... ready to do some serious dine'n.

– The Plan –

Once inside the restaurant, the plan was simple... Maybe?

- Mrs. Older Fella up front of the line, encourage'n 'n assist'n the kids.
- Mr. Older Fella at the rear of the line, keep'n an eye open for "potential interruptions".
- YF and GF casually move'n up 'n down the line modeling quiet chitchat and lots of polite manners.

"Okay. Everybody line up (single file) behind Susie Jo."... And wouldn't you just know!... Before that serve'n line got started move'n real good = red light! Everything just kinda shut down... Uh-Oh...

The "coach'n staff" called a time out and huddled up for a quick *trouble call*. Mrs. Older Fella quickly pointed out the problem that had hindered progress??? The kids were doin' great move'n down the serving line choosing the meal they preferred... the sides and various condiments, beverages–but–at the last stop when the server asked, "And how would you like your steak?"... Four adults listened as the next youngster, with a grimace, wrinkled brow, and a slight shoulder shrug, took a weak guess: "Cooked???"...

Solution: The Young Fella and Girlfriend quickly 'n quietly moved up and down the line and matter-of-factly mentioned to the kids somethin' 'bout, "rare, medium, or well done."

Well, for sure, the Older Fella had stepped in his own dinner bucket. But the Young Fella, being the good guy that he was, said, "But who would have thought...????"

READER REFLECTION: Please refer back to READER REFLECTION... *Shoes*. The *"Huh?"* story highlights a former "Project Kid" (currently a minister) and also a prominent community leader who shared a kindred spirit... plus... both men possessed a thankful heart... resulting in a delightful Easter "*Thanks*-giving" meal for 27 middle school age PEOPLE!... Hmmmmm... Now wonder where those two "Gifters" got an idea like that?

INSIGHT: John 4:35 "I tell you, open your eyes and look at the fields. They are ripe for harvest." (NIV)

10

SURPRISE! SURPRISE!!

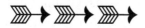

Psalms 36:7

"How priceless is YOUR unfailing love…" (NIV)

11

Surprise - n. Amazement, dumbfounded, shock.
        v. Flabbergast.

READER PARTICIPATION is requested to assist in setting the scene for this delightful little story. Sooooo, would you please:

    A) Visualize a return to 1950...

    B) Picture (in your mind) an upper East Tennessee city, population 150,000...

    C) Envision the oldest (north) section of the city... the community which had initially been the most prosperous district, but which by 1940 had lost that particular distinction, and was now classified as a "blue-collar" neighborhood–but was still known by many as a community made up of "hard-workin' salt-of-the-earth folks."

    D) Finally, imagine yourself in the Happy Holler community of "the Old City" of that town.

Happy Holler was somewhat of an enigma, with the local old timers readily attesting to the legend that "the Holler" was called "Happy" because (in the old days) every other building in the "Holler" was a saloon/barroom!... Leading up to a major point in this story: mommas didn't want their kids in or around the "Holler" after dark. Truth be known, that edict also applied to all husbands. But don't you think, most likely, all towns have their own "Happy Hollers"?!!

Now here is the story for you to enjoy. It was the graveyard shift... almost 2:30 a.m. Things in Happy Holler had finally quieted down. The two officers had positioned their squad car in an area that afforded them a broad view of the Holler, with minimum exposure of their vehicle. The Veteran Officer had only minutes prior reported in (via two-way radio) to the desk sergeant at the City Jail, "...line of vision = three city blocks south; two city blocks north. Zero traffic. Zero pedestrians. All quiet."

Suddenly, the Rookie directed his pardner's attention to a very slow-moving vehicle approaching their position down the hill from the south. Judging from the dim, yellowed glare of the encroaching headlights, the Senior Officer correctly determined the vehicle to be an older model car.

It was apparent to both men that the car had begun to swerve back 'n forth... back 'n forth... back 'n forth.... But only slightly so...'n ever so slowly... a *peculiarly* slow pace. The driver appeared to be destined to be charged with DUI.

After allowing the old car to pass their position–just exactly as depicted in the old crime movies–the squad car pulled discretely into position behind the suspected DUI vehicle, the squad car's red light brighten'n up Happy Holler and the siren sound'n a brief, "URRR". Almost immediately, the brake lights on the old car flashed as the car rolled to a very smooth, complete stop. The car's engine was immediately shut down and the headlights were promptly turned out. Driver co-operation was, at that point, "so far, so good".

The Rookie approached the passenger side of the old, then identifiable, '37 Ford Coupe. Since it was midsummer, the Ford's windows were rolled down. The *age* of the old car is significant to this story because the old model cars all had manual transmissions, the gear shifts often referred to as "3 on the column" or "4 in the floor".

The Veteran Officer, as he cautiously approached the

car, could not get a good, clear look into the vehicle. Just as he was about to order the driver to "Step out of the car!"... Mr. Officer got the biggest surprise of his law enforcement career!

A small nine-year-old towheaded boy said excitably, "This old car is hard to steer!"

Then!!

A second boy, even smaller than the driver, literally "popped up!" from underneath the steering wheel and said, "I work the pedals!"

What a great story!

No READER REFLECTION on this true story. Just enjoy it!

INSIGHT: It's a given: "Two are better than one because they have a better return for their work." Ecclesiastes 4:9 (NIV)

11

A TREAT FOR CURLY

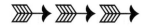

Psalms 51

"Only GOD can supply the necessary purging and only GOD can accomplish total restoration of soul and body from the damage of sin… This (psalm) is the O.T.'s greatest statement of the doctrine of original sin." (Eerdman's Bible Commentary p.483)

Senior - Of or designating the older of two...

Lesson - Something learned... A period of instruction. *An instructional exercise.*

It was the last Halloween of the 1940's and for nine-year-old Curly it was gonna be his most excite'n Halloween ever. Only three more hours 'til dark... He had already secreted away a bar of Mom's soap which she kept in the old pantry. But the boy was completely unaware that in less than five minutes after he arrived home from school, Mother had readily detected that frequent, mischievous demeanor exhibited by her son when Curly was ponder'n on an adventure he knew his folks would consider out-of-bounds.

One more hour and Dad would be home... then a half hour for supper... another 15 minutes help'n Mom with the dishes and then... "Trick or Treat!"... and it was really gonna be a neat TRICK!... Curly knew exactly what he was gonna do, 'cause he had overheard the older boys at school talk'n 'bout this particular TRICK.... This was gonna be "as easy as pie".

So far, so good... dishes almost dried and... Doggone it! Dad shows up, "needn' to talk to you, Curly." Uh–oh... Then the two men of the house retreated to that *special* (??) corner of the room where the senior of the two always invited the junior pardner "to have a seat" whenever there was some serious talk'n to do... and it was serious– Doggone it!... and how did Mom know 'bout the soap? Guess it really didn't matter. What did matter at the time was what Dad was gonna do 'bout it?

One thing 'bout Curly = he 'n Dad had gathered

together in that old corner more than a few times in his young lifetime, and he'd learned a thing or two: to confess his misdeeds, and the quicker, the better... 'cause Dad, have'n been a boy at one time, understood boy stuff a lot better'n Mom understood 'm. So the youngster just said right out and real plainlike, "Uhh, Daddy, old man Copperly is gonna get his winders soaped-up real good tonight."

Mom wasn't the only one in the house that was a pretty good "thinker ahead" 'bout things; Dad could sure do his own share of that kind of figure'n. The senior pardner knew right off why Mr. Copperly was Curly's intended target for a special Halloween TRICK, but he couldn't hardly let his boy know that he knew. So, kinda casual-like, he asked his son just 'xactly what it was that made 'm wanta soap up the local grocery store proprietor's windows? Naturally, the boy explained as best any nine-year-old could explain. And the explain'n of it was that "Old Mr. Copperly was always mean to all the boys 'n girls when the grown-ups were not 'round."... an opinion, then unknown to the kids of the neighborhood, that was shared by most of the adults living in the general area.

Dad just sat a while (and pretended) to ponder up a solution to the problem. Eventually, he told Curly 'bout the Halloween when *he* was ten years old and with two of his buddies turned over Old Mr. Plotnicky's outhouse.... Shoved 'er right over into the creek.... Reason was 'cause Old Man Plotnicky was a whole bunch like Old Man Mr. Copperly in the way that he was always fuss'n at the kids.

The three boys totally wiped out Plotnicky's potty... 'cause that old man was just like *Old Man Copperly*. He was mean to all the boys 'n girls. However, things turned out bad for the boys... and bad for their moms 'n dads. Those three sets of parents had to pay their hard-earned money to build that hateful old feller a brand spank'n new OPF!... outdoor potty facility.... Meanin' that the cantankerous old man came out "smell'n like a rose"!

All of that trouble because the boys decided to pull a Halloween TRICK on somebody they didn't like. And the boys? Well, Curly had to sit a while longer and hear all 'bout it, but that's a story for another time....

Reluctantly, Curly handed his bar of soap over to his dad and concluded that this Halloween was his worst *ever* Halloween. However, his senior pardner gave his boy a big ol' smile and said, "Don't say nothin' to your mom or sis. Be real quiet and slip into your room and get your Halloween outfit on and meet me back here in 'bout ten minutes." Though the boy was somewhat puzzled, he did as instructed and was back in that old, unlucky corner of the house in 'bout five minutes.

READER REFLECTION: For those Readers who are (Baby) Boomers, you will most likely remember durin' that era in blue-collar neighborhoods, most of the kids Halloween costumes were mostly old clothes several sizes too large, or too small, with a handkerchief/bandana or a homemade mask for a face covering.... Just like Curly's "costume" that night.

As Curly was wait'n for his dad to return to "the corner", a strange woman walked into the house through the back door... a woman unfamiliar to the boy... until... she spoke!... It was Dad!... And he had *two* bars of soap!!... one of which he handed to a little boy who, literally, stood there with his mouth wide open....

First thing Dad instructed his son to do was for Curly to lock his little *Rusty Dog* in the basement, 'cause anyone who saw *Rusty* would immediately recognize Curly. Then, the *two* carefully slipped out the backdoor so Mom would not know what was goin'n on.... Or did she!?

READER PARTICPATION: Wanta guess the very last place the twosome visited for Trick or Treating that night? *Right!* And a couple of things the (formerly) curly-haired boy still remembers about that last stop:

#1. The "lady" saying somethin' 'bout her being the tallest, so she would soap the tops of the winders and Curly could soap the bottoms.

#2. No one in the neighborhood ever recalled anything ever being mentioned by Mr. Copperly about his winders.

And one final remembrance of Curly's... which he VIVIDLY recalls–His dad was quick to point out the difference between having to replace a damaged building versus the clean'n of a few, undamaged winders even though the winders may not have been rinsed.

READER REFLECTION: When "re-visit'n" your own younger years of living life with your parents, grandparents, siblings; what similar "lessons learned" do you continue to practice and to value?...

INSIGHT: Matthew 7:12 "Do for others what you would like them to do for you." (NLB) Matthew 7:12 is often referred to as the Golden Rule.... And all grade school children know that anything "golden", especially if it's a lesson learned well, is of great value!

12

SHOE BOX AND GRAYSON

Psalms 69:6
*"O LORD… may those who seek YOU
not be put to shame because of me."*
(NIV)

Texas - A state of the south-central United States.

READER HEADS UP! When the average Joe/Josephine thinks of Texas, most likely visions of Large… Big… Huge are mingled somewhere within those initial thoughts. And for good reason = TEXAS is bigggg country and has been promoted as such even before Davy Crockett's last big adventure unfolded. Accordingly, this little story is about a big, good–ol'–boy–TEXICAN and his small, cute animal critter.… And the tell'n of the story's gotta start by explain' the reason this big ol' feller's momma nicknamed him "Shoe Box".

Well, Baby Shoe Box was born in 1956, 3½ months earlier than his folks had been told to expect 'm. The little rascal weighed in at a full two and one-half pounds!! When Momma *finally* got to bring that little feller home… Yup!… You's right! She literally brought him home in a *shoe box*! However, little Shoe Box being the true Texican that he was/and is, wasn't long spend'n time in that shoe box. When he did hit a growth spurt, he for sure hit a good'n. Eventually he wound up being 6'3" tall and 225 lbs. But no matter their age or stature, it's well documented that many Texans' favorite animal is the horse. However, for Shoe Box, though he liked the ponies well enough, his favorite critters were dogs. BIG dogs. The bigger the better!... And Shoe Box was always a lifelong dog owner.

Now, "fast-forward" from the *baby in the shoe box* to the retirement party of that (now) burly lineman known by his fellow linemen as "Big Poppa". Also, it is pertinent to note that some 30 years prior to that retirement party, the "pole climber" had succumbed to the charms of the little blond

English teacher at the local high school.... Matrimony is the word and Ms. Connie is her name. Additionally, it's helpful to mention that Ms. Connie, through the years, has conferred to family, friends, and the preacher, that she's beginnin' to get more'n a bit discouraged in try'n to teach Big Poppa how to *speak* proper English... say'n she gave up long ago 'bout try'n to upgrade his *write'n* skills....

However, the Missus says that her big ol' life pardner is so good to her that she has always supported his various endeavors and has especially shared his love of big dog critters. As a matter of fact, Ms. Connie was equally heartbroken when, after 14 years of befriend'n his human friends, their big dog moved on to the "Happy Hunt'n Grounds". Most dog owners know that losin' a good canine buddy can oftentimes make folks melancholy–to say the least! And such was the case at the home of the schoolteacher and the big lineman.

It was only a few short weeks after their canine's demise when Mr. Poppa, while mow'n the yard, glimpsed the movement of a critter of some kind dash under the house, right below the kitchen window.... Further investigation proved fruitful...very fruitful. There were *five* critters under the house: one full grown critter 'n her four kittens!

Five cats! Ms. Connie was sympathetic. *Poppa* was irate, immediately threatnin' to "dispose" of all five of his uninvited and unwanted "guests"! Once again, exactly as it first had occurred some thirty years previously, the schoolteacher applied her wistful charms and her big buddy reluctantly granted their "visitors" a reprieve. A near miracle–being that Big Poppa was an avowed dog man who "...hates CATS!"

Nowadays, accord'n to a very reliable lady, should

either family, friends, or the preacher happen to drop by for a visit, be it an early morn sunrise or right 'bout twilight time in Texas, those visitors would observe that big, tough ol' lineman sit'n 'n gently stroke'n a little gray ball of fur, from which emits a soft prrrr'n sound… just barely audible over the big man say'n somethin' that sounds like, "Good boy, Greyson. Good kitty."…

READER REFLECTION: Which part of this (true) story best caught your attention? The baby in the shoe box… or… Shoe Box's conversion?

INSIGHT: Genesis 1:20-25 (NIV)

13

BOGGINS!....

>>>→ >>>→ >>>→

Psalms 139

The Permanence of Divine Companionship!

Maltreat - To treat cruelly. A corrupt practice…

It was only a couple of days into the fall quarter at the local middle school… 30+ students per class… classes changed every 55 minutes… certainly not yet time enough to learn names of new students.

However, roll call that afternoon (5th period) had gone well. (Be nice now in what you're think'n.) Hey! Sometimes even R/C can be challenge'n… plus, student cooperation in completin' a "blended" student information/reading assignment was proceed'n in a surprisingly pleasant manner.

"Mr. Teacher, can I talk to you?" she whispered…. She was a small girl, even for a 6th grader… petite, long blonde hair, rather "unattended"… as was her clothing. Whispering even more softly, "My name is Stephanie. I want to ask you to do something for me."

"Maybe so. What do you need?"

Slowly movin' from the front of the large desk, 'round beside Mr. Teacher's chair… head 'n eyes cast downward, one hand clasped behind her back, the youngster shyly voiced her request: "Would you call me Boggins?"

Mr. Teacher, responding in the manner of any astute adult, answered by–stallin'… "Beg your pardon, Stephanie, but what did you say?"

"I asked if you would call me 'Boggins' instead of Stephanie."

"Well… Uhh… Sure, if it's okay with your Mom 'n Dad. Is that your nickname?"

"Uh-Huh," she answered…. Little did Mr. Teacher know that for the next several years the educator was gonna be doin' most of the learnin' throughout that long friendship… most of which *continues* to be amazin'.

For example, by age seven, Boggins had lived in two different states, various in-law/out-law dwelling places, attended three different schools, and had experienced the death of her best friend/playmate–who was murdered 'n is still an unsolved case…. Unfortunately, by the time of Mr. Teacher's initial acquaintance with this special little gal–abusive adults had robbed her of any true sense of childhood safety and welfare.

It is good that this book is one of short stories…. Perhaps one day Boggins herself may write of her life. However, all remaining comments and "stories" of this determined woman expressed within the pages of this story will be, in her own words, "Positive"….

Boggins' 6th grade year eventually did have some *positive* things happen…. While some school personnel learned of her plight and began to assist… her largest group of boosters was a small group of college students who had "adopted" the kids at that particular campus–wanna guess who one of the favorite kids happened to be?... Yep!

Stephanie was born in August 1970. "Boggins" was *self-created*, years later…. "A name I really liked… from the PBS Kids TV show, *Boggins Hill*.... I now think of it as a way of establishing a new identity for myself." Listen 'n read the words of Ms. Boggins, now fifty years old, as she recalls when she first began to *enjoy life*....

- "When those college people 'adopted' me, I experienced a lot of FIRSTS in my life: *Laughter*! I discovered I had never before experienced *laughter*–I *did not know* how to laugh. It was great!"
- "My 6th grade year, *Marie... she just showed up everywhere... picked me up in *her car* 'n took me places..."
- "And *Turtle... I really loved her too... I'll never forget that Turtle took me to see the movie, *E.T.*... the very first time I had ever been in a movie theater."
- "Whenever 'n wherever I was with that bunch, I was *never* made fun of..."
- "I was always just one of the kids... lots of fun things..."
- "When I was with them, again for the first time in my life, I got to be a normal kid!..."
- "One long weekend they took me to 'camp'... an experience I will *never* forget.... I went with no extra clothes; no sheets, blanket, pillow; no soap, towel, wash cloth... just the clothes on my back.... Those college women tossed me in the shower–*wonder why*?... made me WASH *really* good... then washed the lice out of my hair... and somehow managed to "requisition" various articles of clothing from some very generous middle school age girls...."

- "I also remember sitting around a campfire for the first time... and all of us getting together and making that now famous hobo stew!"
- "Oh–one more thing. That was the weekend that I realized that GOD really cared about *me*– Boggins!"

*Marie and Turtle: Two of the young women who were part of the aforementioned "Booster" group.

That year and a half passed too quickly for young Boggins.... By no fault of her own, various legal issues stemmin' from the previously mentioned "at home" violations of the child's personal safety, the youngster was moved to another community... then, a second time... and finally started high school in *another* adjoining county. Just prior to completion of her freshman year, Boggins was dismissed from school... moved again, out-of-state... to Kentucky....

It was not until she was eighteen years old–and literally homeless–that the young woman, Stephanie, reconnected, by accident?? with a couple of her former "boosters" from middle school. Boosters who still remembered their friend, Boggins! The gracious generosity of a Godly widow immediately took Boggins *off the streets* and for several months provided the needed assistance that enabled the grateful young woman to, once again, *bounce* back!

Try'n to keep this story short, its conclusion will briefly (attempt) to highlight the *Travels of Boggins*...

BOGGINS... on the road again...
- 1970 - Birth to age 5 - Florida.
- 1976 - Tennessee - Ten years in several counties.
- 1986 - Kentucky.

- 1988 - Back in Tennessee at 18 years of age.
- 1989 - Traveled several Southeastern states with state fairs.
- 1993 - Had somehow convinced TN Hwy. Department officials that she was a qualified 'n competent *dumptruck* driver… which she proved to be and was trained to also operate, professionally, the Bobcat and backhoe machines.
- 1995 - Attended night school, adult learning classes, receiving her high school GED. * She *started* these classes with a 5th grade reading level!
- Late 1990's - After checkin' newspaper employment ads, applied for a position–of all places–in Atlanta, GA. After only six months on the job, the woman was promoted to an apprentice-level supervisory position on a major construction project site…. By 2000, the lady had her own work crew of several "finish" craftsmen.
- After a move to Ohio in the early 2000's, this determined personality was, by 2008, employed by J.P. Morgan Chase… in a management position with 106 employees under her supervision.

- And in 2016, Stephanie semi-retired to St. Augustine, FL., where she currently resides in an exclusive subdivision. The most recent conversation with "Boggins" concluded with her invitation to, "Come visit us. We've got a really nice pool. I designed 'n built it myself!"

A Full Circle: 1970 Born in Florida • 2020 Retired in Florida

READER REFLECTION: Most likely, you are acquainted with one who, like Boggins, rose above very HARSH difficulties... possibly, you may even be a "Boggins"... or you may be in a position to be a special friend to one who is currently in a "Boggins" environment?... Sooooo...

INSIGHT: Most folks have heard the story about the injured man lying beside a deserted highway and a Republican saw him and immediately ran away. Likewise, a Democrat hurried by refusing assistance of any kind. NEXT to see the injured man was a foreigner, an immigrant... Obviously, this is a paraphrase of the original story found in St. Luke's Gospel chapter 10 (NLT) Conclusion... "Go and do the same".

14

MULE TALES...
CLIPPITY CLOP, CLIPPITY CLOP...

Isaiah 41:9-10

You are MY servant: I have chosen you... I AM with you..." (NIV)

This pre-story of *Mule Tales* "reaches out" for an extra bit of somethin'... sort of like those little kindergarten folks who have fun doin' their "show and tell" activities.... Or maybe like the Baby Boomers get'n *two* scoops of ice cream on their slice of apple pie. Therefore, the intent of this pre-story story is to call the Reader's attention to the illustration of the cowgal standn' by the big tree at Indian Wells. *An illustration that will be addressed on down the trail... kinda like "show and *tails*".

Indian Wells is the renowned half-way point of the Grand Canyon National Park's mule ridin' experience.... "Going up" or "Going down"... makes no difference to the mules... it's still half-way. However, *all* Grand Canyon trail travelers find Indian Wells to be *the* place of rest 'n relaxation. Uh... well, "relaxation" may not be the appropriate "feel good" word mule riders would choose to use as a *bottom*-line description–if you're using your imagination....

It's almost needless to mention that even the mules 'n birds 'n other such critters could distinguish the difference between the mule riders and the group of *hikers* who had coincidently convened at the famous waterhole. The hikers, attired in lightweight T's 'n hiking shorts; comfortable ultra-light athletic footwear; ball caps and various other up-town headgear; were all *sit'n* around enjoy'n the respite.

Conversely, the mule riders were dressed like the lady at the big tree, as illustrated, and as *required* by the GCNPS: Wide brim hat; large neckerchief; long sleeve button up shirt; belt; blue jean britches; above the ankle boots.

But... as astute Readers have already determined... the lady is *standing* up... leaning on the tree. *Standing*... as were *all* of the riders!! No sit'n 'round for these mule skinners. They were prepare'n for the next 3½ hours of their decent.

Ouch!!!!

Mule - The sterile hybrid offspring of a male donkey and a female horse.

Equestrian - Of or pertaining to horsemanship. Depicted or represented on horseback. One who rides a horse (or mule!).

Sol - The Sun.

Sol's bright smile was especially beautiful that mornin'... as was that of a certain vivacious woman who was smile'n right back at Mr. Sol. Sunrise in America's Grand Canyon is often spectacular! And it was a good sign to see both of'm shine'n so brightly that particular early spring mornin'. After months of anticipation, it was the day when several early mornin' decisions would determine whether or not the woman–along with twenty-two other decern'n folks sit'n in a big circle would either– "Saddle up! Or go get your money back."

The old cowboy preside'n over that little pow-wow did seem to manage a slight hint (maybe?) of a smile as he spoke; but his mood and intent was stern 'n firm: "Folks, this is serious business. It is not an easy trip. People are few 'n far between who are will'n to shell out their hard-earned cash just to sit on a mule seven hours ride'n down a steep trail that's often times not as wide as the mule"... and pointed down towards the bottom of the world-famous canyon. "If you've got any doubts–you need to leave. Right now! No hard feelings."

When the dust finally settled the lady with the bright eyes 'n smile, plus her husband and eight other quiet, tight-lipped tenderfeet were still sit'n in what was left of that big ol' circle... all of'm givin' the old bronc buster/ mule wrangler their undivided attention as he motioned for the remnants of his little "herd" to bunch in closer. While still remain' firm in his leadership role, the old wrangler's sternness subsided... that initial gruffness was gone... he even grinned a time or two... even stated that he was "look'n forward to trail-boss'n you folks on our little ride."

Turns out the old Westerner, in addition to being able to handle most four-legged critters, was also a pretty fair hand at handle'n the two-legged variety. That particular little trait was Mr. Cowboy's ace in the hole. Have'n won his "new hands" over real pronto, the old rascal's next move was to simply introduce the folks to Wally. Wally was an immediate hit with that whole bunch of tenderfooters! Tall, dark 'n handsome. Beautiful, large brown eyes... long legs... all four of'm. Mr. Cowboy then informed his listeners that the GC Park Service always kept 175 fully trained trail-ride'n mules available at all times. All of'm 'specially trained to safely shuffle park visitors in 'n out of the canyon.

READER HEADS UP! Following is the job description/ list of qualifications/"certifications" of a single mule transporter of (mule) riders who choose to traverse down into and up and out of the Grand Canyon, via mule.

Each GC mule must:
- Complete a minimum of *seven* years packing supplies in 'n out of the Grand Canyon.
- Complete an additional *two* years being ridden by GC wranglers while said wranglers conduct guided tours for park visitors.

- Following each mule's completion of the required (minimum) nine years of "apprenticeship", GC park staff/officials review and evaluate the mule's performance. Only when that "apprenticeship" has been deemed a success will that mule then become the most significant part of the team which accompanies park visitors on a breath-taking, unforgettable adventure.

*This one-man's remember'n and paraphrase'n is just that! So, if one hundred percent concise information is necessary, GCP Services should be consulted.

After introduce'n Wally Mule to the newcomers, he then introduced himself… "Just call me Buck." Then procede'n to discuss mules 'n mule safety when decend'n the trail down the canyon walls, Mr. Buck casually mentioned an incentive designed to assure the full attention of his apprehensive tenderfeet: "Wally is not only our oldest mule in the Park Service, Wally is the most gentlest, smoothest walk'n, safest mule in the whole history of Grand Canyon mule ride'n! And while I'm give'n ya'll the ins 'n outs and the do's 'n don't's 'bout the potential hazards of our trip today 'n tomorrow–the *one person* in this group that I see sit'n up real straight, look'n at me real hard and pay'n the most 'n best attention to what I'm talk'n about– that's the lucky person who gets to ride old Wally!"

Upon conclude'n his instructions, Wrangler Buck answered a couple of questions, expressed his own satisfaction that his "new hands" would fully cooperate with all further instructions given, and assured them that the upcomin' two days of adventure would be remembered throughout their lifetime.

...And the Wally winner!...

"Folks, I've been wrangle'n these mules for a lot of years and sure can't remember anyone pay'n attention as good as her."... She was the good-look'n lady with the bright smile.

READER REFLECTION: A word of warning should you be consider'n long distance mule ride'n. Become familiar with how to best prevent and/or treat strawberries! Also, a word of encouragement. Most positive, unforgettable adventures always have a way of makin' "uncomfortable", well worthwhile.

INSIGHT: "Sunrise in America's Grand Canyon is often spectacular!"... is worth this echo, echo, echo....

15

MICKEY D'S

⫸→⫸→⫸→

Isaiah 42:8

"I AM the LORD; that is MY NAME."
(NIV)

Underprivileged - Socially or economically deprived.

Incident - A definite, distinct occurrence.

Story Participants:

- 21 middle school gals 'n guys - residence: public housing, the inner, inner-city
- The Young Fella - early 20's
- The Older Fella - early 40's
- The Ice Cream Lady

Date of Adventure - The week between Santa's annual appearance and New Year's Day, mid-80's.

READER PARTICIPATION: Please slip back into *your* "memory bank" to recall a couple of those weeks between holidays when:

    A. *You* were a student 'n how you passed the time after St. Nick's visit, wait'n for the big ball to drop at midnight, Dec. 31ˢᵗ?

    B. Assume'n you *now* have children of your own, how did/do you manage *their* meander'n through that particular week?... and have you ever wished for a help'n hand? If so, you are gonna 'preciate the good intentions behind this *successful* story....

"Meanwhile, back at the ranch," in the East Tennessee foothills of the Great Smoky Mountains... remember the two fellas mentioned earlier as "Story Participants"?... This twosome was part of a larger team of kid friendly folks in the business of provide'n positive experiences 'n adventures designed especially for middle school age PEOPLE.... And in this case, their plan also happened to provide a "bonus" for several mommas who received an unexpected *kids' day away*.

And the plan?...Simple–Time worn–Usually successful ... get the word out to the kids prior to their holiday break... a brief handout/flyer did the trick.

Example: HIKING TRIP/FREE
Smoky Mountains
Tuesday, Dec. 28th
9:30 a.m. – 6:00 p.m.
Call: (The Young Fella) 123-4567
FREE
Bus Leaves at 9:30 a.m.

Obviously, those of you who "parent" these 11–14-year-old "cookie crunchers" know they need frequent reminders about almost everything = require'n lots of personal contacts... from the "event planners"... who serve to keep kids 'n parents updated. Those various promotions of the scheduled outing proved successful, result'n in 21 mommas enjoy'n their kids' day out.... (That number of moms is correct if there were no siblings among the kids.)

READER PARTICIPATION: Please keep in mind these youngsters were inner city folks... most lived in what some refer to as "the Projects". Now, lots of interest'n and fun events took place on the trip. Many, if not most, folks would be surprised to observe kids see'n *for the first time*: a real log cabin, a crow, a red-headed woodpecker, a deer, and a bear!... with cubs!! However, *this* story is only gonna go into detail about a single incident.... Stop'n at Mickey D's (McDonalds) on the way back home.... Actually, the stop at Mickey D's was not on the "itinerary".... It was a stop of *necessity*... but not unexpected.... After all, with 21 kids on the bus!...

READER HEADS UP! Readers aged 45+ years will remember that at one point in time, Mickey D's sold ice cream sundaes for 99¢... vanilla ice cream with a choice of chocolate or caramel top'n.... And back then, those cool treats were popular with kids between the ages of "1 'n 92"....

So, it was no surprise at all–the surprise would have been had it *not* occurred–when one very *hopeful* boy hollered, "Hey! Let's get an ice cream sundae!" Kinda... well sorta... try'n not to be so obvious... the Older Fella fumbled 'round and came up with $19 and some change; the Younger Fella had $3.... With a few of the kids having enough change between'm, the party came up with enough for the ice cream and Uncle Sam's share... the deal was on.

Only two things remained... Get'n the "order" together and choose'n a couple of kids to go with the Young Fella to help'm carry the goodies....

... UNTIL...

One gal raised that loud chorus of cheers of which 21 kids are capable of when she shouted, "Let's go through the Drive-Thru!!"

READERS HEADS UP! Another reminder for the "mature"

readers and a Heads Up! for the younger folks = back in the day, Mickey D's drive thrus did not have an overhang of any kind.... Customers would drive up to the window... place their order... pay the Order Taker/Cashier 'n wait there for their order.

... Which is what transpired ...

That old bus rattled 'round the building and being the only drive-thru customer at that time, rolled right up to the window, and...

Folks, the look on that window lady's face was... well, it was... just really hard to describe–and that's an understatement at best!

Maybe it was see'n the old bus pull up to her window?... maybe it was the 21 kids all up front, piled in on its driver?... could be that she just couldn't hear the order?... Probably all of the above, plus? But finally, the ice cream lady got the order straight.... It was 19 chocolates 'n two caramels.... And the kids all insisted that she keep the 72 cents in change that they over-budgeted....

Those kids are now "middle age" grown-ups.... And if by chance either of those two "Fellas" ever run into any of them, rest assured that the "...19 chocolates 'n two caramels..." will be mentioned.

READER REFLECTION: Just for the fun of it = take a couple of minutes and put yourself in the place of the window lady/cashier when that old bus rolled up. What might have been your reaction(s)??

INSIGHT: Compassion is oftentimes synonymous with kindness... *Loving – Kindness!*

-

16

REMEMBER'N MOM

》→ 》→ 》→

Isaiah 43:1

"I have summoned you by name: you are MINE." (NIV)

READER HEADS UP! *Remember'n Mom* was a letter written to Mom as a CHRISTmas gift, Dec. 2000.

REMEMBER'N   MOM…1915 –
                   Fatherless at eleven
                   Child of the Great Depression
                   Young bride
                   (Soon) a young MOM –
                   "Sister" born in '36
                   Little brother arrived on –
                   The heels of Pearl Harbor.

REMEMBER'N   The hard times; lean times; good
                   times!
                   Dad, the breadwinner –
                   Mom, the "warm spot" in the home
                   and literally, the HOME maker!

REMEMBER'N   The good food–always! And always
                   enough… and who did the cook'n?

                   Cook'n was (and continues 2 be)
                   Mom's "thing"

                   And where did that food come
                   from?

                   Well, it was never fully appreciated–
                   then –"Thanks, Dad!"

REMEMBER'N   The clean clothes–and who did the wash'n?

Washday was Monday

Washstand–tubs–ringer washer–clothes pins

…And who did the iron'n?

REMEMBER'N   The cold mornings

And race'n to the small coal stove in the kitchen

That other warm spot –

With the warm shirt hang'n above it!

Who built the fire every morn'n?

And how did that shirt get there?!

REMEMBER'N   The winter nights

Water heat'n in the big kettle

On the little stove–and sponge baths! Brrrrr...

REMEMBER'N   The fun times:

"The Lone Ranger!"–on the radio

Television? Folks on Oldham St. had hardly ever heard of it!

(And never got one until the newness wore off)

Fox and hound!–kick the can–
neighborhood badminton!

Croquet tournaments–and rook in
the winter…

YEP! And sit'n in Mom's lap–"year
round!"

REMEMBER'N

The old green rocker

And sit'n in Mom's lap and Mom
sing'n "I got spurs that jingle,
jingle, jangle…"

But the thing most remembered is:

Mom whistle'n–Mom was the very
best whistler in the whole world!

Bar none!

REMEMBER'N

Mom teach'n me to tie my shoes–
what a chore!

Teach'n me to read –

Take'n me to town on the streetcar!

And fix'n soft-boiled eggs when I
was sick….

REMEMBER'N

With a smile, now –

All those switches Mom kept

On top of the old refrigerator…

Now why would Mom do that?

Today, it most likely would be described

As a "strong-willed child express'n a difference of opinion with one in authority"

But Mom's reaction–as I remember, was always to grab one or two of those switches

The little woman–4'11" could do this without break'n stride

Grab the switch(es)

And nimbly pursue the object of her opposition

All the while shout'n in a clear, raised voice,

"I'm gonna get you–you LITTLE DICKENS!"

"MOM,"

Thank you 4 love'n me all these many years. I LOVE YOU too!

Merry CHRISTmas Dec. 2000, "Little Dickens"

ADDENDUM:

REMEMBER'N MOM II
By: L. Dickens
Nov. 2019

REMEMBER'N   After Dad's Death
Mom's 67 year – Life Companion
…gone…

REMEMBER'N   The Little Lady's Firm Resolution
To continue living in their old homeplace
…alone…

REMEMBER'N   Mom's "stiff upper lip" while
deal'n with her loss 'n loneliness –
still retain'n her sweet smile.…

REMEMBER'N   Mom's warm, unfailing hospitality
shortly after enter'n her home –
"Can I get you anything?"

REMEMBER'N   When Mom could *not* remember as well as in the past,
but birthdays often have that particular effect
…even for Moms…

REMEMBER'N · The sound advice given by understand'n, care'n friends:

"...laugh often, even when you do not feel like laugh'n, or else you will cry frequently."

REMEMBER'N · The bedtime prayer Mom taught us early in life:

"Now I lay me down to sleep, I pray the LORD my soul to keep.

If I should die before I wake, I pray the LORD my soul to take."

And my 88-year-old Mom at *her* bedtime –

Now pray'n that same prayer– again–with her "little" boy.

REMEMBER'N · However, Mom did make one slight (?) adjustment:

This precious little woman would always *conclude* the prayer –

"I pray the LORD my soul to keep!"

REMEMBER'N · That was not the way–the *word*– Mom taught us!

It just didn't rhyme.

Look'n back, Mom was right.

"Keep" is the correct word.
Mom is a "keeper"... John 14:1-6

REMEMBER'N

A mom's last words to her son…
that afternoon at the hospital!!

Mom, just a couple of minutes from
heaven, unable to speak above a
faint whisper and with her life-long,
curling back and forth motion of her
index finger – beckoning……….

Her boy bent close to her – as she
whispered her *last* words to him:

"i…love…you" – and then, a
second time! "i…love…you"

REMEMBER'N

Her son's *last* words – to his Mom –
"I LOVE YOU, MOMMA!"

POSTSCRIPT: *Remember'n Mom* was written to Mom as a CHRISTmas gift, Dec. 2000. Two years later, and one year prior to Mom's death, she *finally* relented–somewhat–about my being such a "Little Dickens!" Her comment: "You were not *really mean*–just very *mischievous*."

L. Dickens

"No one is poor who has a Godly mother." (Abraham Lincoln)

17

A CRYSTAL-CLEAR SOLUTION

Micah 6:8

"...the LORD has already told you what is good, and this is what HE requires: to do what is right, to love mercy, and to walk humbly with your GOD." (NLT)

Arrogant - Overbearingly proud; haughty.

Exaggerate - To overstate or enlarge something disproportionately. Hyperbole.

Win - To succeed in gaining the support of.

STORY PARTICIPANTS:

- 85+ Junior High School Guys 'n Gals
- 10 Community Service Volunteers
- 5 (put in the middle) Store Managers
- 1 Regional Store Manager

This story took place in the 1970's in Hard-Working Blue-Collar Community, U.S.A., maybe in a community such as yours.

READER HEADS UP! This story is only one of dozens of the adventures experienced–'n now enjoyed!–by the ten original volunteers who were striving to be positive role models and establish meaningful friendships with junior high school PEOPLE.... A story of young adults seek'n to encourage young teens to consider develop'n the social and moral values of CHRISTianity–becoming a good neighbor and a good citizen....

It was a beautiful autumn in Southeast U.S.A. School had been in session since the Monday follow'n Labor Day. An average of 85+ junior high schoolers had begun meet'n together on a weekly basis... one night (Tuesdays),

7-8 p.m.… in an old, free stand'n stone building utilized mostly for storage space… but it "cleaned up" good; and being stone, proved to be a near perfect site for JHS kids to congregate.… Just wasn't much there for them to damage… and those ten young adult organizers* seemed up to the task of plan'n *and* conduct'n all sorts of *positive* chaos.

*Please note that start'n right here, let's refer to those ten organizers as "the Young Folks" – while still refer'n to the young teens as "JH Schoolers". (Don't forget now…) "Thanks!"

The Young Folks had "recruited" several of the older JH Schoolers to "join up" and help build their new club. Several of these young teens were eager to contribute their ideas 'n time… and proved especially capable of: 1) "get'n the word out" and 2) "recruit'n' their friends 'n classmates to join them… at "Club 7-8 p.m. every Tuesday night at the Band House." Winning the support of the JH Schoolers was akin 2 take'n "One Giant Step Forward".…

Keep'n in mind that most parents were vigilant as to the whereabouts of their young teenagers, what do you think happened next?? If you guessed somethin' 'bout moms get'n involved, kudos to you!

Not sure whether or not Mom's Day Out had taken hold in the 70's, but can attest to the fact that Mom's Night Out just seemed to naturally take hold 'n evolve as MNO began with moms car-pool'n kids to 'n from club.… However, it did not take long for the moms' ingenuity to kick in: drop the kid(s) off at 6:45 - pick'm up at 8:15 and 1½ hours for: the beauty shoppe; dinner/supper out!; grocery shop'n; and how 'bout simply enjoy'n some good *ol' peace 'n quiet*?!… Regardless, in gaining the moms' support, it was "Take'n One (more) Giant Step" forward.

So far, so good... for the carpool kids, but what about the walkers? Those gals 'n guys who walked to their club (and school). Without these youngsters, the tell'n of this little adventure would never have taken root... And as the story unfolds, it is kinda amuse'n (positively so), that these walkers became the *envy* of most of the riders! How so?

Well, that's pretty easily understood once one considers the community in which that junior high school was located: an older (residential) neighborhood... only three *short* blocks from a major thoroughfare/business district in a fairly large Southern City... lots of kid friendly "attractions".... And certainly not lack'n several fast-food options.

READER REFLECTION: Should you be a former walker/ commuter from your own school days, you will recollect that traverse'n *several* city blocks presented no problem whatsoever for "walkers"!... You will also remember what *you* would have done–or did–when you were in JHS and had opportunity to hang out with your peers... socialize'n with the pretty gals/cute boys at the local hamburger joint. So, it's not at all surprise'n that the walkers began congregate'n every Tuesday night after their Club meet'n... soon to be joined by the riders... 'n yep, you guessed it: like clockwork, over one half of those 85 JHS kids, on their special night, descended on their favorite hamburger joint! All the new customers naturally pleased store management, who began to add two–three extra employees to welcome and serve the Tuesday night *crowd*. And things were workin' out great. It was a good deal for all those concerned.

Whopper - A story. A tall tale.

Condiment - A seasoning for food, such as mustard, ketchup, may-o, salt, pepper, etc....

At this point in this particular whopper, it should be called to the attention of non-Boomer readers that the few franchised H/J's of the 1960's and 70's served as the forerunners to the almost countless 21st century H/J's... meaning that the Boomers 'n their kids could actually have it their own way when trim'n out their burgers via various condiments placed on each individual table.

And if you are smile'n right now you're get'n ahead of the story... because you are probably guilty of what you are smile'n about!

Keep'n in mind that those 60's and 70's fast food H/J's were of a kindred spirit in feature'n some very colorful, color-coordinated décor–via the plastic dispensers that burger *con-o-suers* found to be very advantageous when strive'n to maximize their own efforts to fully *condimentalize* their burgers.

For Example:

- Ketchup was dispensed when the customer put the squeeze on the red plastic (ketchup) container.
- Mustard = ditto the ketchup dispenser with the obvious difference being yellow (versus red).
- Salt and pepper were readily recognized by the white (salt) 'n black (pepper) shakers....

And you're smile'n again, you rascal!

Now back to that previous reference about the store managers of the H/J that was the recipient of those junior high schoolers spend'n Mom 'n Dad's hard earned $$ and how pleased those proprietors were to have that new business... for about three months!... Until some of the normal and to be expected 13–14-year-old teen behavior started to surface. Nothing bad, mind you... just an occasional ketchup (screw-on) top drop'n off the bottle when adult customer(s) were squeeze'n out some of that particular condiment on their fries.... Or maybe salt come'n out of the pepper shaker and/or vice versa.... Or some JH schoolers simply stand'n 'round after they had made their purchases, which seemed troublesome to adult *enterees* 'n *exitees* by obligate'n them to take a few extra steps one way or another.... Or require'n of them a few seconds of their time?...

A couple of "Tuesday Nights" later, it happened.... A 10 p.m. phone call... to the senior volunteer of those young adult friends of the JH school youngsters.... Ring, Ring, Ring. Yep, it was the H/J callin'.... And rather than a request, it was a demand that the recipient of the call "hurry down" to the restaurant... "ASAP"....

"Sure–be right down."

Upon his arrival (at the H/J) the senior volunteer was hustled off to the office... located in the rear of the establishment.... It was a very small office... furnished only with a small desk 'n desk chair... and a single, even smaller chair set'n in front of the small desk... it was very crowded.... Kinda like squeeze'n into a five o'clock, *goin' home-time,* elevator on a hot day.

Five store managers of various ages 'n sizes, everyone of'm wear'n the traditional white shirt feature'n the restaurant logo just above the shirt pocket, had surrounded that little desk... all of'm look'n real *serious like* at their visitor.... But not as stern look'n as the very chunky, red-faced, middle-aged man hunkered down in the chair behind that little desk! His stern "Have a seat, sir," caused the visitor to recall memories of similar instructions from years ago, a personal visit to the principal's office. Well, at least the visitor got to sit down.

"I have been South-Eastern Regional Manager of *blank* Restaurant Systems for over 20 years. On one occasion in my management career, Atlanta, GA stores were experiencing similar disturbances as these being acted out by your junior high delinquents. Those troublemakers were members of the Hell's Angels bikers!... And I personally put a stop to that problem.... And if you people think this company is going to tolerate that kind of behavior by a bunch of rowdy teenagers who continue to disrupt the business of this store, you are mistaken. Now, what do you have to say, Mr. Visitor?"

It was suddenly very quiet in that small, crowded room when the visitor slowly rose from that chair... Smiled... Gave a slight nod of his head towards the attentive store managers... And very politely addressed Mr. Southeast Regional Manager prior to departing the premises, "Sir, it's great to hear how successful you were in your dealings with the Hell's Angels. It's sure a relief to know that you'll have no problem deal'n with these neighborhood kids."

READER REFLECTION: Reader Friend, were you the one who switched out the S 'n P shakers, or the one who just *kinda* loosened the top on the ketchup bottle???

INSIGHT: Haven't we heard somewhere, something about throw'n rocks at people–and how to determine just who it is that's gonna toss the first one?...

18

"CAN YOU FIX MY CHICKEN?"

John 1:1-5

The Pre-existence of CHRIST!

Pet - An animal kept for amusement or for companionship.

Story Participants:

- Tess Whiteside - Mom in Charge
  - Composure never disrupted
- Eddie Whiteside - Junior high student
  - Newspaper Carrier
  - Poultry Associate
- La La Whiteside - Baby Sister
  - Family Princess
- Ms. Wanza - Next Door Neighbor
  - Think/sing/hum "Like a good neighbor..." You get the idea...
- Dr. Chumbly - Neighborhood Veterinarian
- Herman Whiteside - The Chicken

READER HEADS UP! The following story is a great example of how attached folks can become to their pets–be it the "animal companions" have two legs, four legs, or no legs... be them canine, feline, hoofed, reptile, aquatic, or fowl–it makes no difference. Animal people and animal pets, to say the least, can become best of friends... as confirmed by this (1957) story of Herman and the Whiteside Family. Accomplished readers will immediately detect something a bit different about the family's choice of names for a chicken... like she (the chicken) had a rooster's name... and that *Hen*rietta, pun intended, may have been more fittin'....

Young Eddie was a conscientious teen who worked as

an employee of a local newspaper, contracted to deliver the daily paper to customers who lived in the residential area where Ed's family resided. In addition to being an enterprizin' young fella, Eddie was also a bright 'n engage'n student... one who always earned honors on report cards and garnered "extra credit" on various projects when such incentives were made accessible = extra effort which provides the grass roots of this very funny story. A story that begins with this young student seek'n "extra credit" on a particular science project.

The semester-endin' project offered many and various options to students in which 10–12 hours of extra study and preparation could yield grades of A's 'n B's. Young Ed opted for a project that promised *maximum* extra credit... never realize'n that his decision would soon result in extra enjoyable moments 'n memories for the entire Whiteside family, and one particular very sad memory. And the science project selection?... Eddie Boy chose to join the time-worn debate of "Which comes first, the chicken or the egg?"

The young man soon discovered that much research was required to undertake such a project. Some folks wondered if Eddie Boy had "bit off more than he could chew". Be that as it may, the youngster remained unfazed. Too much to get done: How to build an incubator? (By utilize'n a five-gallon metal lard can.) Proper wattage for the light bulb? (20 watts.) How to secure the proper fertilized eggs? (The aftermath of this part of the project was when the young chicken farmer learned that he had indeed misnamed his chicken!) How many eggs needed to start the project? (12 eggs. *Herman was the sole survivor.) Incubation period? (21 days before Herman's arrival.) Finally, a proper "residence" for baby chicks would be needed. (A wooden crate filled with straw was Herman's abode... for a while.)

After Herman's successful hatch, and with Dad Whiteside work'n long hours, and the older siblings have'n already flown the coop, new Poppa Eddie, Momma Tess 'n the family Princess proved to be little Herman's primary "caretakers".... Especially Tess... Being the official "Mom in Charge" and the one person who spent *by far* the most time with young (Miss) Herman, Tess soon disposed of the wooden crate which had "confined" their newest family member. (Miss) Herman soon had the run of the house... which was smack-dab in the afore mentioned residential section of a rather large city.... Ahemmm...

READER HEADS UP! 21st century folks would simply refer to (Miss) Herman as a "lap chicken"... and (s)he would be right at home with all the other pigs, snakes, lizards, fancy-named *weezels,* and such *varmits*... or, uhhh... "lap pets". Regardless, (Miss) Herman soon proved to be a privileged member of the Whiteside family.

Shortly after the CHRISTmas holidays and some three months after the chicken's comin' "out-of-the-egg-party", the local weatherman ordered up a big cold snap that included... "lots of ice and up to five to seven inches of snow." But Eddie Boy had always adhered to the neighborhood postman's policy of "Neither rain, nor sleet, nor snow." Bring it on! And sure enough, Mr. Weatherman's prognostications of "100% precipitation..." of snow proved to be fact.

Late the next afternoon, the young entrepreneur, after

trudge'n through that heavy snow to deliver the daily paper, returned home hungry, wet 'n cold, and very tired. Mom's kitchen was welcoming, warm, and cozy that particular late afternoon. And young Ed was especially appreciative of Mom help'n him remove his snow 'n ice-packed galoshes. Boot removal was move'n along at a fairly good pace until Momma Tess, hurry'n to assist the youngster in the dispersal of the slippery, cumbersome rubber boots... inadvertently... stepped backwards. Uh-oh! The family never really ascertained whether or not poor (Miss) Herman had come to help in their time of need–or was simply a curious, innocent bystander??

The Paper Boy and the Mom in Charge were stunned... speechless... (Miss) Herman's demise was instantaneous. But the young Princess, a first grader, was the only person to acknowledge the chicken's fate. "Momma, Herman's dead. His neck is broken."

After what seemed to have been a long period of time, the always stoic Momma Tess finally spoke to the Princess. "La La. Hurry! Go tell Wanza that we need to take Herman to the doctor!"

"But Mom, his neck is broken. It's like this." She mimicked, with her neck extended crookedly over her shoulder... eyes closed... mouth wide open... All to no avail.

"La La. *You* go tell Wanza we need to go to the vet. Hurry! Tell her I'm on my way to her house!"

READER HEADS UP! At this point in the story, a few additional comments are needed:

1) The Whiteside family did not own a vehicle.

2) Wanza, their next-door neighbor was:
   a very good person,
   a good friend,
   had a great personality,
   accommodating,
   middle-aged,
   pleasantly plump,
   most always dressed in a "Moo-Moo",
   a chain smoker.
3) Wanza's car was a 1948 Pontiac–with a "great big" steering wheel. She was a slowwww but safe driver.
4) Also, for some "un-remembered" reason, Eddie, the newspaper boy, neglected to accompany the three ladies when they rushed off to secure professional medical care for the now *crooked neck* chicken.

Since the date of (Miss) Herman's demise was in 1958, the sole reliable source of information about *this particular part* of the story is to be seen through the eyes of the (then) six-year-old Family Princess... an account that today, is a very humorous, vivid eyewitness account... especially when demonstrate'n the chicken's broken neck, and her momma's very subdued and unusual demeanor when address'n the doctor.

"The trip itself was really kind of fun. Momma had wrapped the chicken up in a bath towel... Wanza had the old Pontiac warmed up. She was smoke'n her ever-present cigarette 'n wear'n her ever-present Moo-Moo, but she did have a short coat on. It was very cold and start'n to get dark. Someone had put snow chains on the old car and

I still remember the 'crunch, crunch' of the ice; and how slow Wanza always drove. And how she always had trouble *turning* the great big steering wheel when she went around corners....

"When we finally arrived at the vet's office, the staff was in the process of locking the doors, but the office manager recognized it was an emergency and admitted us. And before the doctor could see us, Wanza had managed to fill the small waiting room full of smoke. Seeing Wanza sitting there in her Moo-Moo enjoy'n puffing her cigarettes was quite a contrast to Momma's sad countenance while sitting there holding her dead chicken.

"Then the doctor walked in and asked Momma, 'Mrs. Whiteside, what has happened?' Very gently Momma unfolded the towel and very softly spoke those few words that our family so fondly—and not without lots of laughter—remembers.

"Doctor... Can you fix my chicken?"

"And I also recall the words spoken by a understanding, sympathetic doctor. 'Mrs. Whiteside, there is nothing anyone can do. I am so sorry. Your chicken is dead'."

Throughout the years, when (Miss) Herman's story is retold at the Whiteside family gatherings, the Princess' concluding words are always the same– "It's the only time I ever saw my mother cry."

READER REFLECTION: Sometimes/oftentimes, the bond between animal people and animal pets can...

INSIGHT: Good neighbors, and especially good *neighbor friends* enRICH a person's life!

19

FISH'N WITH MY DADDY!
(I FINALLY GOT TO GO!)

St. John's Gospel
1:12; 1:14; 1:16; 1:29... (NIV)

Father - A male parent. A male ancestor.

Daughter - One's female child. A female descendent.

One of Uncle Bud's all-time favorite stories is a story told by a young college student to a group of middle schoolers.... The story of her *first fish'n trip*....

Seems as though the soon-to-be first grader really had a difficult time understand'n just exactly why her older brother was the one who *always* got to go fish'n with their dad.... It wasn't fair! Just because she was a girl. She wanted to go fish'n with her daddy. Just him and her... nobody else. And then one day, her wish came true. Dad was gonna take her fish'n... just the two of 'm! Follow'n is the account of the *picture* Ms. Tina painted with animated words 'n gestures that enabled the children to visualize see'n a dad 'n daughter go'n fish'n–*together*!

Fish'n. Laugh'n. Enjoy'n a real "goin' fish'n lunch"– which Mom had packed especially for her fishermen. Laugh'n some more and reel'n in the fish! All of which were caught, with one exception, by Dad. On that special day it did not cross the little girl's mind why a big man like Dad needed so much help *from her* in get'n all those fishes reeled in and put on their stringer?... There were one... two... five... eight ... Fun! Fun!! Fun!!!

With exaggerated enthusiasm the young woman told of the *one* fish that she actually did catch. "All by myself. It was *this* BIG!" she said, hold'n her hands some two feet apart... and gradually inch'n them closer 'n closer together until she held up her forefingers some four-five inches apart. Obviously, she had caught the children's undivided attention. "And when it was time to go home, my daddy taught me how to skip rocks across the top of the water. He said since we were leave'n it would be okay to scare the fish away."

Like most little kids, Tina wanted to *carry the fish*. Reluctantly, Dad agreed to let his young daughter carry the stringer of fish back to the car. Reluctantly, because the path lead'n back to the car was, at one point, steep and narrow. Very close to the water…

It was not that the young daughter was unwill'n to take heed of her dad's words to "be careful…" she was just extremely excited. She had zero intentions of goin' for a swim! Carefully and softly, Tina encouraged the children to: "Picture yourself as a six-year-old, fall'n off a high bank into water over your head, and it's easy to understand that I thought I was going to drown!… Until my daddy reached down and very gently pulled me *up 'n out* of the water."

She then told how *disappointment* quickly replaced the fear she experienced when, safely out of the water, she realized that she had lost their (stringer of) fish! And Dad?... Well, neither the loss of the fish nor his daughter's unplanned dip dampened his enthusiasm for the delightful outing they had experienced on their "first fish'n trip" together. A trip both daughter 'n dad would remember for a longgg time–evidenced by Tina's retell'n of their story many years later to a group of middle school kids.

In conclude'n her fish tale to those attentive kids, Tina mentioned that as a young adult, she now understood the reason her dad had waited to take *her* fish'n was a safety precaution. She ended her fish'n story by saying that ever since the day her daddy had "fished her out" of that deep water, he had always been her best friend! Tina stated that she knew her dad *loved her*, "More than anybody in the whole world... Except JESUS. And JESUS loves all of you as much as HE loves me and my dad."

READER REFLECTION: Reflecting back on your own childhood, what memories do you visualize of a special adult–family member, teacher, coach, Sunday School teacher, neighbor?? who "structured" a specific activity, outing, field trip, weekend, or "fish'n trip" that brought fun, laughter, enjoyment, and delight into your growing-up years. A special person who could also help to calm your emotions of fear and disappointment. And let's not forget about the pleasant memories that, as an adult, you personally experienced as you remember the faces of those children to whom you have *passed it on.*

INSIGHT: This Daddy/Daughter story especially brings to mind another, much older story. "Friends, have you caught any fish? Throw out your net on the righthand side of the boat and you will get plenty of fish... Bring some of the fish you have caught... Now come and have some breakfast." John 21: 5-6 (NLT)... WOW!!!
"JESUS loves me, this I know, for the Bible tells me so..."

FISH'N WITH MY DADDY!(I FINALLY GOT TO GO!)

20

CHRISTMAS... AT HOME???

John 3:3

"I assure you, unless you are born again..." (NLT)

Home - The place where one resides. A family living in a dwelling. To the center or heart of something; deeply.

Sol - The Sun.

December 22nd 1963… "Blizzard conditions."

December 23rd… "More snow on the way. Sub-freez'n temperatures… ice!"

Oh no!… Tomorrow is CHRISTmas Eve…. And it's nearly 400 miles from Fort Bragg, NC to Hometown, Tennessee…. No way to make it home for… better just forget it….

Doggone the military anyway! The emotional stress of serve'n in Uncle Sam's Army often proves to be the most difficult of the many demands placed on the shoulders of Uncle Sam's Soldiers… and especially in the mind of a soldier's wife… which seems to quadruple durin' the CHRISTmas holidays… at least for this *particular* young Army wife who had never before missed being "at home" for CHRISTmas. And no! She did not want to hear the old cliché 'bout "There's always a first time…" But really… Well, so much for saving up all that leave time….

Unexpectedly–and pleasantly surprisin'!–the 24th day of December dawned with ol' Sol smile'n big 'n bright and as the early mornin' progressed, Sol kept shine'n brighter 'n brighter! Temperatures warmed up considerably (well, somewhat), and the weather prog-nost-to-caters promised "Ice free roads and good drive'n conditions" for at least 150 of those 400 miles towards Tennessee.

READER HEADS UP! At this point in the story, it seems of some importance to mention that Mr. 'n Mrs. Soldier–

should they decide to "head homewards" would need to make adequate room for a couple of additional travel'n companions. Although these newcomers would have no say in any of the decision make'n, the twosome's inclusion within the proposed winter wonderland excursion would significantly impact the venture.... Venture?... Uhhh... Hindsight certainly suggests that "adventure" should be the more appropriate term....

The decision to *Go!* was a "no-contest" determination for this military-minded couple. They not only shared the same last name, the same bed, and the same matrimonial "rank", they also shared a deep hanker'n to be home for CHRISTmas! (Oh yeah. They also shared a close personal bond with those two previously mentioned newcomers.) *Hurry 'n pack!*... Their plan was simple. Travel as far as possible. Turn back only if conditions proved to be too difficult. Obviously, such potentially hazardous experiences for this young couple had been few. And "hazardous" was not a concept that had fully developed in their minds... and barely in their vocabulary. "Shoot! It's CHRISTmas! The folks are expect'n us!"...

The soldier and his bride pooled their financial resources ($28.73 would buy plenty of gasoline in 1963), and hurriedly packed the old car, being very careful to leave adequate space in the back seat so the mattress from the baby bed would fit snugly... with some room for a couple of stuffed toys, diapers 'n baby bottle stuff, and extra blankets... no problem. Plenty of room for both the *sixteen-month-old* toddler and his *four-week-old* Baby Sister. "Eud'n, Eud'n, Eud'n"... the old Ford was warmed up good and ready to go. "Move out!"

READER HEADS UP! 2020 Google Search states the distance between Ft. Bragg, NC and Knoxville, TN to be 370 miles via I40, and requires six hours non-stop travel time. In the early 1960's, I40 was non-existent in the East Tennessee/Western NC area, and the trip required eight to nine hours travel time.

One distinctly hazardous stretch of road was the sixty miles between Ashville, NC and Newport, TN. The high mountain road was punctuated by the numerous road signs depict'n sharp curves; dangerous curves; warnings; loops. However, the greatest danger to travelers on that section of highway was the high volume of "tractor trailer trucks" which literally ruled that stretch of the *two-lane* mountain road!

A travel trip ticket for such a trip would look something like the following:

Depart Ft. Bragg, NC

Destinations:

Sanford, NC

Asheboro, NC

Salisbury, NC

Hickory, NC

Morganton, NC

Marion, NC

Black Mtn., NC

Asheville, NC

Hot Springs, NC

Newport, TN

Knoxville, TN

And for that military family travel'n home for the holidays?... Well, on Dec. 24th, 1963, those weather prog-nost-to-caters' prog-nost-to-cations were right on the money. Actually, much better! The first 200 miles were, for the most part, light-snow drive'n... just taking things easy... not much traffic either.... That little 4-door Ford sedan was doin' good. Little over halfway home... then another 50 miles up the road, but not snow free.... Hummmmmmm... The snow was get'n deeper... no problems as-of-yet... not much traffic at all. After click'n off another 30 miles and stop'n to "gas up," Mrs. Soldier noted that "There's a lot more snow up here in the mountains. And it's getting colder..." Soldier Boy simply nodded in agreement and made no comment about the ice he had noticed that had formed under the snow.... Two hundred and eighty miles behind them... almost to Ashville and then those tough 60 miles to Newport. It sure was a good thing that Mrs. Soldier was on such favorable speaking terms with the Good LORD!

Include'n hitch-hike'n, the Soldier Boy had made that trip over 'n through those mountains several times... but never when there was virtually *no* traffic on the road... not even a tractor trailer! However, there was evidence that a few of those big rigs had negotiated that old road at some point after the snowfall = it was those big tracks the little Ford followed. Travel was very slow... on a few occasions it was necessary for the little Ford to be backed up several yards in order to gain sufficient momentum while climb'n a steeper grade.... Only one time did the young soldier have to come to a complete stop in order to "let some air out" of the rear tires.

Eleven hours after depart'n the safety of Ft. Bragg, NC, the trustworthy little Ford's ignition was turned off... right in front of Grannie's house!... A small (?) CHRISTmas miracle for a young military family–still remembered! And should one happen to push "fast forward" to December, 2022... 59 years later... one would find that old soldier 'n his bride reminiscin' about the year they *almost* missed being *home* for CHRISTmas.

POSTSCRIPT: That *reminiscin'* has become an annual holiday tradition that began many years ago when two older 'n (somewhat) wiser "adults" recalled that particular holiday experience. They decided that STUPID was the proper define'n word to best describe their lack of sensible judgement in '63. They now simply refer to the decision as *dumb*!!

... And today ...
Prayers!... for safe travel that snowy 1963 CHRISTmas

Eve were both heard and answered! And throughout the years, especially during the CHRISTmas season, the young, *now old* couple continue to express their amazement 'n "Thank YOUs" for the wonderful memories of the LORD's Presence during that young family's "casual, ho-hum, uneventful" and amazing CHRISTmas adventure!

21

SUPER HERO DOWN!... ERRR, UP!

John 10:28

Absolutely No Snatch'n!

Dedication - To set apart for some special use. To commit (oneself) to a particular course of thought or action…

This little story is a funny tale that demonstrates the *extreme stunts* that a group of dedicated youth workers incorporated when planning a "Super Hero" camp weekend for 200+ middle school age PEOPLE….

The plan was to *"jump start"* the fun 'n excitement, in twenty minutes or less, upon the kids' arrival at camp. Twenty minutes after step'n off the bus and drop'n their luggage at assigned cabins, the kids would personally greet 'n meet their *Super Hero*!... Their guardian 'n protector who would shield them from any perceived harm from any 'n all bad guys, and lead the way for each kid to experience a weekend they would remember for many years to come.

READER PARTICIPATION: This is one of those stories that "you had to be there" in order to receive maximum smiles 'n laughs. Probably it will enhance the humor of it by imagining that you were sit'n in on this particular planning meet'n…. *Please note that a camp director's responsibility entailed total camp activities, while the program director's responsibility entailed MC'n various games, skits, and fun activities throughout the weekend. Now back to the planning meet'n….

Almost immediately, when the role of program director was mentioned, three people *in unison* suggested that Bubba be invited to serve in that capacity…. "All in favor… Unanimous! Bubba's our guy!"

And no wonder: Bubba's great personality… Bubba loved kids and kids loved Bubba…Bubba had served as PD on several occasions in past years... an outstand'n young man. Also, it's important to mention that Bubba, a former high school defensive tackle, would *not* look out of place as an offensive lineman at a South Eastern Conference school. A point to *remember* as this story continues.

Bubba was very excited at the prospect of another opportunity to help "entertain" the kids and personally attended the remain'n planning meetings. And for whatever reason, Bubba was adamant about which Super Hero that he was gonna portray.... Are you ready for this?... Spider-Man!! All two hundred 'n fifty pounds of him!

Initially, the above-mentioned poundage appeared to be a, a well, a, a hinderance in his portrayal of Spider-Man... until someone realized Bubba had a hilarious idea. Then the newly declared Hero casually mentioned that, as of yet, he had been unable to find a "size-able" Spidey suit... for himself.

Surprisingly, one of the young men on the PC mentioned that he had such an outfit... "Guaranteed to *fit all sizes*, and Bubba was welcome to use it." This young man was taller than Bubba but not as *filled out* as the soon-to-be Super Hero. The PC, upon hear'n that this particular costume was made of a new stretch material that (as previously mentioned) *fits all sizes* = "Game On!" And only those folks serve'n on the plan'n committee knew what was gonna happen at camp... or did they?

Fast forward to Friday Night Camp... 200+ kids 'n 60+ college age young adult counselors filing into the large rec area, sit'n on the floor, ready to "jump start" the weekend. Time for the PD to make his initial appearance... well, almost time....The two fellas help'n Bubba get "in costume" were not exactly set'n record time–nor even scheduled time...But finally...Spider-Man was ready to make his appearance.

Rewind this story back to when Bubba had arrived at camp a couple of hours prior to all but work crew folks. Bubba had previously fashioned several small, *odd-shaped* blocks of wood that when secured on the rustic wooden walls of the rec area, were virtually unnoticeable. Utilize'n wood screws and a battery powered drill, our Hero had positioned the blocks of wood in such a way that would allow him to *cling* to the wall... a la Spider-Man. And as attentive readers would expect, his *handholds*'n *footbraces* were not very high up on the wall because Bubba's vertical jump was that of an offensive lineman.

After Spider-Man's big introduction...

After Spider-Man's personal "Welcome to Camp"...

After a few words of assurance that he, Spider-Man himself, would be with them the entire weekend to guard and protect them...

The Hero asked for complete silence as he would then demonstrate some of his unique skills. The lights dimmed. Complete silence. And exactly as planned, Spider-Man raced across the room!... jumped!!... and REALLY did cling to that wall!

It was AMAZIN'!... All were enthralled!... It was unusually quiet... UNTIL...

Rippppppppppppppp!!!

It was not known until that night that everyone's *Super Hero*, Spider-Man, wore bright red gym trunks!

rippp

MORAL OF THE STORY: Manufacturers have yet to develop a material that *one-size-fits-all*... and much more important, such *unveiling* events are the kind of things that make camps for kids so much fun... and make great memories *for many years to come!*

22

TESSIE

≫→ ≫→ ≫→

John 14:23

"If anyone loves ME he will obey MY Teaching. MY FATHER will love him, and WE will come to him and make OUR home with him." (NIV)

Tessie was born:
- in 1922
- in a two-room structure
- in rural Kentucky, coal mine country
- in a family of six
- the youngest of four children...

Tessie never knew her alcoholic daddy. He was shot dead!... before she was born... shot right off the seat of a mule-drawn wagon... by an irate husband. Her mother then placed the four children in an orphanage in Lexington. And simply walked away. The baby girl was three months old.

The children's mother only returned to the orphange on four occasions—when each child reached thirteen years of age—at which time that child was taken from the orphanage and placed in a questionable 'n suspect form of "indentured servitude". Tessie's two older sisters worked at various assignments in mining towns. Her brother was "rented out" to a large farming operation. True to form, in March, 1935, shortly after Tessie's thirteenth birthday, the mother arrived to claim her remaining orphan.

However, the mother's fourth 'n final trip to the orphanage proved to be vastly different from her previous trips. She was confronted by a young teenager who had absolutely no intentions of being "farmed out", as had been the fate of her siblings! Tessie's determined resolution to remain at the "Home" prevailed. In later years, as Tessie reflected back on this particular incident, she stated that "GOD had already worked things out for me to remain at my *home* in Lexington."

Evidently so! Odd Fellows Home in Lexington, KY served as the young lady's guardian home until her high school graduation... her becoming a licensed beautician... and assisted her to gain full-time employment at a beauty salon in a small, neighboring town. Tessie's first "public works" job! The year was 1940... the young lady was eighteen years old and on her own... and once again, as fate would seemingly have it, this very special young woman was not destined to be "on her own" for very long.

Tessie's "instant like" personality immediately gained favor among many of the salon's clientele... a truth not at all surprising given the fact that this young lady's care, concern, and repect for others was so obvious.... Plus, the young newcomer's work ethic also proved to be another asset. One regular client in particular was so impressed that she arranged for her unattached, 21-year-old son to "Come and meet that cute young woman!... Her name is Tessie."

He did! He also agreed with his mom's accessment of that cute young woman!... so much in aggreement that he asked Tessie for a date... three months later Jack asked Tess for her hand in marriage... *She did!*

Eleven months later..... Little Miss Perfect arrived..... Oct.,1942.

Twelve months later.... Jack, Jr. appeared................ Oct.,1943.

A "leap year" later....... Little Eddie arrived............. Oct.,1945.

It appears that October was somewhat of a significant month for the young couple.

Three children in four years obviously served notice that Tessie no longer had time to work at the beauty shop. So guess what? She assumed all the shop's business provided to them by–ready for this?–local funeral homes! Once again, Tessie's determination and mental toughness had shone through. In March of 1953, the arrival of the Princess ended both the Octoberfest of baby arrivals and of baby arrivals period. Two girls and two boys. Just the right number.

Shortly after the arrival of the Princess, Jack's small grocery store business fell on hard times. Extended credit to many customers who failed to pay their accounts proved to be financially disastrous for the little store. Forced closure and debt obligation settlements to suppliers necessitated a major change of life for this family of Blue Grass natives... Kentuckians moving to Tennessee!... Ouch!... For everyone but Tessie. Tessie had not only survived tougher moves, but had prospered. Just one look at her family was all the proof she needed. "Let's go! Tennessee, here we come."

Jack had accepted a position in a large grocery store in Knoxville, Tennessee. He was glad to get the job, but forget Big Orange Country. His blood ran Kentucky blue and always would. Tessie, however, was color blind. She had her family to care for. First order of business after find'n a (rental) home was to find a church home for her family. Those two things accomplished, Tess decided to start taking in sewing... which she did for the next 45 years! Consider'n all those years the couple's collecitve means of provision and care of 4 healthy, happy children... 9 grandkids... 15 great grandkids—such success is not anything less than amazing!

In the 1920's and 30's, the accumulation of possessions was not an option for orphaned children... and Tessie was certainly no exception to those standards. Possibly, that may be why Tess was a life long "low maintance" person... and maybe, that is why at the time of her death in 1997, she owned very few personal items. She gave most everything away!

Tessie simply just did not desire a lot of material "stuff". Taking care of her family was her daily goal. Serving those she loved made this special woman happy 'n content. And it would be difficult to even "guesstimate" the number of "chocolate hamburgers", apple pies, and "Tessie's Famous Homemade Rolls" she baked and gifted to countless friends, neighbors, church folks, mail carriers–just whomever!

Tess had mentioned that her job at the "*Home*" was "working in the kitchen... And we had beans every day." (It was really something to watch Tessie eat a *cold* bean sandwich for lunch–one of her favorite sandwiches.)

Tessie's story could go on 'n on and *Tessie Part II* may be in the future. However for now, this Part I rendition will come to a close.... But not before a few "Tessie Tales" are recalled:

Tess was a long-time smoker.... A Lucky Strike gal... lots of funny stories about her smoking... especially about how, after her open heart surgery, the means in which she acquired her Luckys; and the care she took about when 'n where to smoke; and to what extreme she would go to fabricate stories (lie) to her kids about no longer smoking.

And fabricating stories—she once told her Oct., 1945 son, that he was adopted. He was eight years old at the time—and Tessie forgot to tell him any different for several days.... When one of her Grandkids told her she had "pretty legs", she told them that was why she had formerly been a Rockette... danced at halftime at the Dallas Cowboys' home games. Never told them any different; most of them were in junior high school before they realized....

Playing cards *fairly* was also one of Tessie's trials. Simply stated by *all* of her family: "She cheats!" And her kids all declare that "Tessie taught *my* kids to cheat at cards." However, she was very honest about her tendency to cheat. Even gave everyone warning before the games started. Everyone wanted to be Tessie's partner because she always won.

Tessie's children all adored their mom and continue to cherish their memories of Tessie:

On their birthdays... "That day we got to do whatever we wanted; Mom cooked whatever we asked; baked our favorite cake; and we didn't have to take a bath!"

What children wouldn't cherish the memory of a mother who was:

"Devoted to her family"

"Provided a CHRISTian Home"

"Always fair"

"An excellent example of loving people"

There's so much more to be written about this delightful woman, her husband Jack, and her family's admiration of their Mom 'n Dad. Two loving, hard-working parents always serving others.... The children are still amazed that Tessie 'n Jacko were able to provide so much to so many... thrived on blue-collar, minumum wages... never–ever–owned a car... were married over 16 years before being able to purchase their first home!

READER REFLECTION: The last two paragraphs best express this story....

Tessie would repeat the same convictions she had growing up in the orphanage in Lexington, "GOD knew what HE was doing..." TESSIE was the lady's special name. And her real name...

The headstone at her gravesite reads:
TENNESSEE MAYS – WHITEHEAD
March 13, 1922
Nov. 8, 1997

INSIGHT: Which part most likely "mirrors" the story of Your Mom?

23

KNOCK – KNOCK!...

1 Timothy 2:5

"For there is one GOD and one Mediator between GOD and man, the Man CHRIST JESUS..." (NIV)

Volunteer - To enter into or offer to enter into an undertaking of one's own free will.

Safeguard - To ensure the safety of. Protect.

Welfare - Health, happiness, and general well-being.

This narrative suggests a READER HEADS UP! at its very beginning: READERS BEWARE!... Be forewarned... An English professor's worst nightmare. It's not just the fractured sentences 'n unorthodox punctuation–this is one of those Humpty Dumpty tales 'bout, "All the King's horses 'n all the King's men who couldn't put ol' Hump back together again."

Knock – Knock!... is a fun story 'bout two fellas build'n a friendship, and affords some entertain' read'n. However, it's the sincere voice of a delightful *young woman* that makes the read'n of this story especially worthwhile. SHHHH... Listen as she speaks with a kind and gentle nature that defines the storyline... and plucks at the heart strings of the Listener!

To further preface this story, it must be mentioned that the three key individuals depicted in the narrative are all "team players", and representatives of and participants in an organization founded and dedicated to serving the needs of middle school age PEOPLE.

Also, it is necessary to state that prior to becoming a volunteer leader serving the above-mentioned youth organization, each prospective leader is required to successfully complete various staff interviews, board screenings, and a criminal background investigation to assure the safety and welfare for all concerned.

Discombobulate - To throw into a state of confusion.

Chaos - Total disorder or confusion.

By now, as a Reader, you most likely are experience'n a bit of discombobulation, but it's okay 'cause help is on the way–before things become chaotic. One more effort to further your understand'n of this story. Some things just gotta be mentioned that you already know to be a great concept/method/tool/vehicle to assure positive social mingling among middle school age PEOPLE 'n young adult PEOPLE. "Right? YEP!" Been 'round forever... Great kid-friendly stuff for kids of *all* ages! Some examples: hiking • canoeing • tube'n (water or snow) • tower climbing • white water rafting • spelunking • panning for gold • rock climbing • back packing (day trips or over nighters) • fall, winter, spring, summer camps (retreats) • participation in community service projects = learning to *give back*!... Now that you "get it", get ready to read about it. It's Storytime!

Knock - To strike a blow. To make a pounding noise. To bump.

Juvenile - Not yet an adult. Immature.

Delinquent - Failing to do what is required. To leave undone.

Now meet the three *Team Players*.
- K.B. - Age 11. Middle school student. 7th grade.

- Dave - Age 21. College student. Junior year. Major: wildlife management.
- Heather - Age 19. College student. Sophomore year. Major: creative arts.

The Middle Schooler: K.B. the boy with the big smile!… dark brown hair 'n eyes… kinda on the slender side… full of himself, sometimes to the point of being "hyper", but was fairly well-behaved (even though he could *push your buttons* on occasion…) adventurous with a touch of "the rascal" in him–a really good 'n enjoyable fella!

The Two Young Adults: Heather 'n Dave were two of many capable, reliable, and dedicated young adults who so wonderfully chose to befriend some special PEOPLE who were in the difficult process of trying to navigate themselves through that confusing journey known as "the middle school years", years that oftentimes were very trying, discouraging, and lonely for an untold number of children. Therefore, it is significantly noteworthy to state that *adults* have *not* "cornered the market" on getting stressed out! Stress targets people of all ages! Hummmmmm…

READER REFLECTION: Remember, please, a couple of your own applications "for work"… be it a paid position or a volunteer position… and consider what your answers were as you read one young lady's response to the question asked of her: "Why do you want to volunteer your time and energies to serve middle school age girls 'n boys?"

Reader Friend, get ready to meet a real stress – buster! A young woman, with a willingness to venture back into that stressful world of middle school PEOPLE, whose primary focus was centered upon middle school aged girls!

The young woman's response to the specific, complex question, was classic!! A lofty, steadfast response which, to this day, is so richly valued within that particular middle school ministry.

Ms. Heather's response: "Because their world is turned upside down right now and is not very clear to them. I want to help them better understand things so they can make right choices…. I wish that such an opportunity had been available to me 'n my friends when I was in middle school. It was so hard." Reader Friend… are you listen'n for those heart strings?…

KNOCK – KNOCK!…
… Continues with Dave 'n K.B.….

Summer is over. School is back in session… Heather's sophomore year… Seventh grade for Friend K.B… Junior year of wildlife management for Friend Dave. And for whatever reason, the college man, the middle schooler and his parents agreed together that Tuesday nights 6 p.m. to 8:30/9:00 p.m.-ish would be a good time for K.B. and his young adult friend/"Designated Driver" to check out Mickey D's, Pizza Hut, the Krystal or other such venues where Dave 'n his fellow volunteers had planned to congregate while overseeing their "collection" of 11–13-year-olds… as their "charges" zipped down the (small) children's slide at Mickey D's… or assisted the police officer at the Krystal's drive through lane… or anxiously watched as a half dozen youngsters ran to retrieve an elusive golf ball at the local putt-putt course. Imagine having all this fun while still hav'n to make sure their "entrustees" were home by nine…. Such was/is the life of a volunteer/designated-driver of middle school PEOPLE!

And believe it or not, Mr. Dave viewed his Tuesday night outings as 90-95% enjoyable. His very active young buddy was a great kid… full of himself (in a positive way)… very cooperative… minimum stress for the *young* man. Had Dave kept a journal describing his Tuesday night outings that specific school year, those memories *may have been* described as follows:

Week #1 Tuesday night
- 6 p.m. picked up K.B. (at his house)… Met Bill, Heather, Sherri at Mickey D's.
- H 'n S brought two girls each… everyone had a fun time. No problems.
- K.B. was at home and knock'n on door at exactly 8:48. Next week meet at Broadway Pizza Hut.

Week #2 Tuesday night
- Description of outing…
- K.B.'s mom opened door at 8:49… *waved at me.

Week #3 Tuesday night
- Description of outing…
- K.B. was knock'n on door at 8:47.
- Dad opened door… no wave.

Week #4 Tuesday night
- Description of outing…
- K.B. knocked on door at 8:52… *Nobody at home…*
- Dropped by *my* Mom 'n Dad's for a while…Back to K.B.'s 9:58…Mom at door. She waved.

Week #5 Tuesday night
- Description of outing…
- K.B. knocked on door… a repeat of week #4.
- Nobody at home.

Week #6 Tuesday night

- Description of outing...
- K.B. knocked on door. *Another repeat.*
- Nobody at home.

MMMMM... Mr. Dave was concerned... Should he speak with the boy's parents or contact his advisor at the (youth organization) office? The young man chose the latter option.

Turns out Dave's advisor was a long-time friend of K.B.'s family... and was initially surprised by Dave's dilemma.... Eventually, the mystery dissipated when Dave answered his advisor's specific question about the *doorbell*. "The doorbell? They don't have a doorbell. K.B. always *knocks* on the door." Suffice to say that the next afternoon found the Young Man visit'n with K.B.'s mom. She had answered the door as soon as she heard the *doorbell ring*.

...Fast Forward Thirty Years...

Should those folks familiar with the original *Knock-Knock!* story have occasion to bump into K.B.–currently a *captain* of the local fire department–the captain will greet the person(s) with his same old contagious smile... turn sideways... simulate knocking several times on an imaginary door... turn back around with arms *spread, palms up*... tilt his head kinda sideways... and shrug his shoulders. And all present will enjoy a great laugh together.

Bonus Story - June 2021!

Recently had a brief chance encounter with Captain K.B. at the local post office and after a demonstration of his old *Knock-Knock* routine, someone happened to (finally) ask Cap his reason(s) for scheming for extra time with his old Designated Driver buddy.... (Readers will remember Dave's major in college... wildlife management. Also, during the summer months Dave worked as a park ranger in the National Park System. One of his major responsibilities was to demonstrate for park visitors the in's and out's of the various snakes found within the park system. Snakes. Many of which Dave kept in the off season at his parents' residence.) "I always liked to play with the snakes! And there were two that I really liked...."

READER REFLECTION: So...What's *your* favorite "the joke's on you" story?... It would sure be fun hear'n a couple of'm....

And thanks! for your patience with this one.

INSIGHT: Simply remember Heather's *kind* and *gentle* nature. Two of the nine "gifts" recorded in Galatians 5:22. (NIV)

24

THE SAILOR and THE G. I.

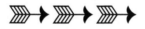

1 John 1:9

"If we confess our sins, HE is faithful and just and will forgive us our sins and purify us from all unrighteousness." (NIV)

Part I

Two baby boys! "Pearl Harbor babies", born in January, 1942... shared the same hometown... lived in neighboring communities. Although their stomping grounds were not hardly close enough to allow *the boys* to attend the same elementary school, *the boys* got better acquainted–and became friends–in junior high school.

In high school, *the boys* not only were football teammates, but both teens spent part of their junior season sidelined by disabling knee injuries. And as is *par-for-the-course* among high school graduates, the two friends went their separate ways afterward.

Shortly after *the boys* completed high school, differentiating world politics, particularly the Berlin Wall Crisis, dictated that Uncle Sam seek additional military personal to serve the U.S. of A.! One of *the boys* volunteered to serve his country via the sea. The second volunteered to serve by land 'n air. Fortunately for all military personnel, a degree of common-sense diplomacy was issued forth from international heads of state, eventually diffusing *that* world crisis, and thus avoiding combat warfare.

Upon completion of their required tour(s) of duty, the two *young men*, upon returning to their hometown, again chose separate paths. The sailor became a successful entrepreneur and businessman. The G.I. eventually *landed* in the field of community service... which is how the two men became reacquainted–after 20 incredibly *fast* years had passed.

PART II

The reunion of the twosome occurred one winter evening when the former paratrooper was a guest speaker at a local church congregation which was interested in learning (more) about a relatively new program/ministry designed to befriend and serve exclusively middle school age PEOPLE. (A local church which was home to a certain former Navy man…)

Following the presentation, and after the crowd had thinned out, the G.I. noticed a man standing back and off to the side of the sanctuary… a man with a familiar grin. It was the sailor! Whoopee!! The two old buddies traded family updates 'n phone numbers and scheduled lunch the next week. However, before depart'n that night, the sailor extended his hand for the last handshake of the night… only… the G.I. noticed… it was a wobbly, somewhat clumsy effort by his friend. With both of the sailor's hands enclosing the G.I.'s hand, and a *hushed* whisper from Mr. Sailor… something about, "… just between the two of us…" So the G.I. dutifully complied with his friend's request and shoved the contents of whatever it was down deep into his pants pocket. And left the "mystery" there… without voicing a word to anyone until the next evening. That night he reluctantly spoke to his wife about the *handshake*.

Turns out that the contents in his pocket, once removed, were ten strips of green paper. And printed on each piece of that green paper was a number: one hundred/100. While Mrs. G.I. was practically turning cartwheels, the old soldier was speechless–*Still is*… when remembering his sailor friend's gift. A gift that enabled a fledgling, thus far successful youth program to, as an old sailor might say,

"Stay afloat". A gift that preceded many other gifts from his ol' seafare'n friend... To mention one other in particular: introduction to a highly respected 'n successful law firm, which "adopted" that particular youth organization.

Much more could be stated about the Sailor by his G.I. buddy... However, the only thing the old swabbie would have had to say concerning his generosity would be found in Scripture passages such as: Psalms 100:5 "For the LORD is good. HIS unfailing love and faithfulness continues forever." (NLT)

READER REFLECTION: This story of one man's generosity can *now* be told to others, because the sea has given up the sailor to the Heavens far above. Also, it must be stated that the eyes of the sailor's old G.I. buddy "watered" up a few times... in the tell'n of this story.

INSIGHT: "Remember this: a farmer who plants only a few seeds will get a small crop. But the farmer who plants generously will get a generous crop. You must each make up your own mind as to how much you should give. Don't give reluctantly or in response to pressure. For GOD loves the person who gives cheerfully." 2 Corinthians 9:6-7 (NLT)

25

LINK

》→ 》→ 》→

1 Peter 5:7

"You can throw the whole weight of your anxieties upon HIM, for you are HIS personal concern." (J.B. Phillips)

Anxious - Worried about some uncertain event or matter.

Worry - To feel uneasy about some uncertain or threatening matter... to feel anxious, distressed, or troubled.

In this story, Readers are gonna meet:
- Link/Mr. Hallmark - College student, age 21-22
- Hubbell and Trouble - Link's two 12-year-old buddies
- Mom - She belongs to Hubbell
- The Biker - Hmmm...
- Mr. Shuffler - The storyteller

It was mid-summer... mid-week... mid-afternoon... a perfect day to be outside in the wide-open spaces hang'n out with a bunch of kids. However, that grow'n stack of paperwork had been neglected far too many times already.... "Pay me now, or pay me later..." (Is "later" better than procrastination?) Anyhow, it was later... and time to make payment.

Therefore, that paperwork day had been one of uneventful necessity for the fella generally referred to as a staff person.... One of two or three folks responsible for the welfare of a group of select college students, who in turn, were responsible for the welfare of a large group of middle school age PEOPLE... all of whom were participants in a youth program designed especially to help meet the various needs of preteens/early teens....

The paper shuffler, confined within his small office, was diligently reduce'n the size of the pile of those previously neglected papers when suddenly, the enjoyable silence erupted in a barrage of hard, rapid blows on the (office) door!

READER PARTICIPATION: Have you ever stopped to consider the considerable differences... those dissimilarities 'n varieties... the bold loudness versus the gentle softness... the uniqueness of a knock on your door? Hmmm...

Now back to our door knocker... "Come on in," offered the paper shuffler, not unaware of the unusualness of the rapid, loud knocknockockockock'n. The visitor quickly openedenteredclosed the office door!... Was that impromptu, fidgety young man stand'n there... Link? Yep. It was Link all right.... Except, Link was *not* all right.

Link was one of those previously mentioned college student volunteers who (at that point in time) was work'n real hard at big-brother'n a couple of 7th grade boys... who throughout this story will be referred to as Hubbell and Trouble.... The college man could best be described as look'n like one of those TV actor fellas the gals watch on the Hallmark series: A clean-cut, nice-look'n fella of some 21-22 birthdays... six-foot tall, give an inch one way or another... probably 180-85 lbs... broad shoulders 'n slim at the hips... dirty-blond hair 'n light-colored eyes. Also, it's important to this story to note that Friend Link always appeared as just have'n returned from "catch'n rays" at some tropical beach; but not so on this/that *particular day*. On the contrary!

The tanned beach boy *look* was gone... replaced by a pale, pallid appearance... Or as Grannie would have declared–correctly–"Boy, yore as white as a sheet!"... and that's not all... the always tranquil young man was obviously unnerved. Finally, he spoke... only three words… "I'm in trouble."

A few moments after convey'n the fact that he was "in trouble", Link hastily replied, "The Hell's Angels are after me!!…" Upon which, Mr. Shuffler promptly locked all doors 'n pulled the blinds. Just jokin'… But Mr. Link was one super-serious young man.

READER HEADS UP! You are gonna laugh… 'cause it's funny now… but for a couple of days a certain young college student's personal comfort level registered "extremely uncomfortable" on the Richter Scale…. And know'n as how you, Reader Friend, are curious 'bout how the Hallmark Man stumbled into his particular predicament, here's his explanation…. (Link did gain a certain degree of composure as he explained his story):

Hubbell, one of the boys whom Link had befriended 'n big-brothered for several months, would surely have benefitted from living in a "more positive" environment…. The youngster was 12 years old…. His (single parent) mom was 27 years old and "not unattractive". (Reader Friend if you are get'n ahead of the story you need to know ASAP that Mr. Hallmark was always quick to deflect compliments 'n even quicker to depart the premises when stop'n by her home to pick-up Hubbell... and always picked up Trouble before pick'n up Hubbell... and *doubled* his caution when he overheard the boys mention that Hub's mom had recently started get'n real friendly with one of the bikers from that motorcycle club previously mentioned in this story....)

One day Hub just matter-of-factly said somethin' 'bout over-hear'n Mr. Biker ask'n his new sweetheart (?) if she knew where Mr. Hallmark lived... Not surprise'nly, that was the day Link came "a knock'n"!

Well... in close'n out this true story, Hubbell's mom and Mr. Biker soon after parted company... Mr. Hallmark's tan returned... and there's only enough space left in this short story to mention that Link, Hubbell and Trouble spent lots of time together for almost two years.... The boys frequently talked about the fun times with Mr. Hallmark.... Many of their trips together were to their favorite creek... where they would catch a bunch of crawdads/crawfish... clean'm real good... boil'm in a kettle of hot water... 'n enjoy their "meal" together!

READER REFLECTION: As sure as my name is Uncle Bud, that's the honest truth... never tasted 'm, but personally saw it happen three or four times.... Bet *you've* probably got a story to equal the crawdad story? Huh?... Trivia question: How many crawdads does it take to feed three grow'n boys?

INSIGHT: What's that story about folks needing to be positive examples for children?...

And... These days, when folks address good 'ol boy Link... they usually address him as "PASTOR".

26

THE LAST "HONEY DO"

John 15:15

"...apart from ME, you can do nothing." (NIV)

Procrastinate - To put off doing something until a future time.

Innovate - To begin or to introduce something new.

Homemaker - One who manages a household, especially a housewife.

Story Participants:

- Mom/Mrs. Honey
- Dad/Mr. Honey
- Curly/The Honeys' eleven-year-old son

The old home-place was built 'round 1900. Just prior to WWII, the cistern and the outhouse, which had served the family well for over forty years, was "relocated"... moved... INSIDE!... simply by enclose'n the old back porch. Indoor plumb'n 'n city water had transformed that old house into an *almost* full-fledged indoor facility. It was a BIG deal! And in 1956 the PPP (plumbin' 'n privy project) was completed with the addition of an honest-to-goodness hot water heater. Ya-hoo!

The next appreciable home improvement to the old home-place was the professional (?) installation of a guaranteed-to-work coal-burnin' furnace... a big ol', good-lookin' piece of *furnuisance*... but shiver! shiver!... that old house still remained *air-conditioned* in the wintertime!

It's now time to meet Mrs. Honey/Mom, a dyed-in-the-wool HOMEMAKER in the truest sense of the word. The model American wife 'n mother of the 1940's and

50's. One who *literally* exemplified what it meant to be a HOMEMAKER!

Mrs. Honey was that person within her family responsible for put'n the SWEET in the Home Sweet Home picture displayed in the family kitchen. Mom was the "brightest spot" in the family, that especial warm place within the sticks, stones, mortar, and flesh 'n blood of her home… *the* single most person who did so much more than her fair share to mold her family together.

Thus, when a homemaker is so invested in family 'n home, most folks would agree that it would be fair that such a lady would be justified to have a "honey do" list. Being so entitled, Mrs. Honey *did* have a Honey Do List, albeit a very short list. Certainly, it was not a list of grievances or complaints, but rather a hopeful request. Seemingly, an *annual* request for her husband's help: "Please, *Honey Do* something about the bathroom ceiling."

Now, Dad Honey was a quiet, thoughtful fella… a really good man who took care of his family… but maybe not always *when* or exactly *how* Mom Honey thought/ expected a project should be done. Anyhow, whenever it was that Mrs. Honey would on occasion choose to make mention of that *embarrass'n ceiling in the bathroom*, Mr. Honey would always say somethin' 'bout, "Nobody's ever look'n up while in that little room." or "It's most always kinda dark in everybody's potty room, so it doesn't really much matter."

So, it happened late one spring… in the early evening… right after supper, that Mr. Honey invited his boy Curly to join him in one of those father-son conversations that always got the son to figure'n just what it was that he had done that was gonna get him in trouble? Besides… it wasn't really an *invitation*... neither was it a *conversation* 'cause Dad did all the talk'n. But it sure could'a been a lot worser... consider'n it turned out that Curly wasn't in trouble after all!

Mr. Honey was need'n the boy's help and cooperation. What was soon gonna take place was to be kept "secret"... just between the two of'm... Dad needed Curly's assistance in put'n up a new ceilin' in the bathroom... a surprise for Mom... and Mom was (later on) *sure* surprised!

READER REFLECTION: Assume'n you are a Reader who reads between the lines and kinda puts things together, then you have already figured out that for the Honey family, having lived in the old part of town 'n such, any new or extra fix'ns of any type were often hard to come by. However, in no way did the environment diminish the happiness and joy experienced by this family. In fact, various difficult circumstances often enhanced their family life. So please grasp the humor in this very amusin' true story. Thanks!

READER PARTICIPATION:
  A) You are being asked to give some forethought about Mr. Honey's innovative think'n of a solution to his problem concern'n that ceiling.
  B) And do you consider Mr. H. to have been ahead of his time?
  C) Please picture in your mind one of those soft cardboard molded containers that modern fast-food restaurants utilize as a means to carry four to six fountain drinks in a to-go order.... Got it? Okay. Hold that thought as this story concludes.

Seems that Mr. Honey had visited a couple of Ma 'n Pa neighborhood grocery stores several days prior to this father-son confab and had asked the grocery men to save their *egg cartons* for him… egg cartons which in the 1940's 'n 50's were made of the same type of soft material as discussed above.

Shoot! Those new ceilin' tiles were light as a feather and with just a little dab of glue on'm those little rascals went up real quick… annnd… with hardly no effort at all they could be trimmed to fit almost perfect. Sure made a nice look'n job… or so the two Honey Do men thought.…

And *Mrs.* Honey? Well, the title of this story…*The Last "Honey Do"*… fully explains what *Mom* thought of Mr. Honey's *egg-asperate'n* undertake'n!

READER REFLECTION: Guess this one's gonna be a split decision… a hung jury… 'cause some folks don't keep anything they don't need… and other folks never throw anything away. So who knows?… Think you are gonna keep those Burger Queen fountain drink holders? You may need'm sometime.

INSIGHT: On a serious note: There's a really special story of a highly successful homemaker found in the Book of Proverbs Chapter 31:10-31. (NIV)

27

A Very deLIGHTful Dog

Philippians 3:20

"See you there!"

Delightful - Greatly pleasing.

Beau/Suitor - A man in the process of courting a woman.

Story Participants:

- The Beautiful Sister - Sis, age 16
- The Hopeful Beau - Bo... The Man with the Dog.
- The Little Brother - Curly, age 7
- The Dog - Flash... Breed...Unknown...

READER HEADS UP! Get prepared to enjoy a fun, very true, story. Circa:1949 U.S.A. A story that needs absolutely no embellishment nor enhance'n because it's a story that has "played out" in countless families throughout the generations... Probably, even within your family.... A funny, human-interest story, unique only in the nature of the bribe that the recipient coveted... and the cost the victim was (finally) will'n to pay....

So begins a story that will–now!–bring a smile or two to all older sisters who had to endure 'n tolerate the younger brother who just naturally assumed that "Sister's" sweethearts who showed up at the old home-place were there to see *him* too! And in Curly's case, the little rascal had more than ample opportunity to co-entertain many young men because his *Sis* was a truly beautiful girl—a "Teen Queen!"—before that term became popular years later. Also, the fact that his Sis preferred to "play the field" increased Curly's chances of befriend'n several additional callers.... Actually, the term "Little Rascal" is most generous... Curly's mom often addressed the boy as "Little

Dickens"....

As the story unfolds it becomes obvious to the Reader why Little Brother became so anxious to be the *first one to the door* when hopeful boyfriend Bo called upon his Sis. One would probably agree that at seven years of age, little boys would not be very knowledgeable as to the merits of "good catch" potential boyfriends when viewed from the eyes and thoughts of young women. However, Bo was one young man who, for a few months, was a regular caller on Curly's sister. Interestingly enough, it was somewhat strange that ol' Bo pretty pronto became Curly's *favorite* visitor... Hmmm....

At first, Bo being the youngster's favorite of Sister's many suitors was a mystery to the family. Bo did not play 'round with the boy like most of Sis's other boyfriends. No toss'n a ball. No horseplay'n. No push'n Curly in his old wagon... what in the world was goin' on?! Ol' Bo wasn't a good-look'n nor a friendly or an athletic guy. No special outstand'n traits. On the contrary, Bo seemed to be kinda socially numb.... But Bo was still Curly's favorite *Beau Caller* because it was Bo who always had that odd look'n little dog with him–always!

Now that little dog was somethin' else! And Curly never ceased to be amazed at get'n to see it.... He even named it "Flash". Curly figured that dog to be just a little bit short of being half as long as a nickel Tootsie Roll.... It wasn't too big 'cause Bo carried "Flash" on a gold chain, snapped 'round his belt.... He always carried it on the left hip side.... Seems what most excited Curly 'bout that dog was that right back of the dog's rear-end, just before you got to its tail, on each of its sides was a kind of a hole.... And you'd put your thumb in the hole on one side of that dog, then put your first finger in the hole on the other side and when you squeezed'm right hard, that little dog's nose lit up! Needless to say, Curly spent almost as much time visit'n with ol' Bo as Sis did... 'n that was a problem... for ol' Bo!

At first, Mom 'n Dad did not understand exactly what Curly was try'n to tell'm 'bout that odd little dog. Finally, Sis explained to'm 'bout Bo's dog.... Unknown to Curly, Sis had also enlightened her parents as to why she had casually told little brother that it was "Okay for him to come squeeze the dog whenever he wanted to!"... Obviously, Little Brother did not comprehend why Sis didn't mind his frequent "pop-in" visits when she was sit'n 'round with Bo.... Nor was he pay'n much attention when he overheard his folks talk'n 'bout Sis only being interested in Bo just so her 'n her girlfriends could go ride'n 'round with Bo in that big ol' four door car....

Well, evidently ol' Bo had deciphered things out somewhat and had decided it was time to make his move. Seems as though Bo had worked out a *sure-fire* scheme that would guarantee some real 'n prolonged *time alone* with the girl of his dreams. The target date: the upcomin' Friday night. The big night arrived and so did Bo–a few minutes early just as he had planned. Sure 'nuff, that curly-haired little brother opened the door before ol' Bo could say, "Scat!"... And for the first time ever, Bo unsnapped that gold chain that held Flash on his left hip... squatted down right low... and hold'n up that dog... square in front of the surprised 'n suddenly silent youngster.... "Curly," says he, "you really like my dog, don't you?"...

"Sure do, Bo."

"Well, Curly, how would you like to *have* this dog? –to

keep!"

One might well imagine how BIG that little kid's eyes got!... and how he could hardly swallow... and started fidget'n 'round. "Oh boy!" he said and reached for Flash. But Bo was not yet ready to surrender his dog.

"Curly, you've got to *promise* me one thing."

"Yeah! Yeah! Okay! Bo, I promise. I P.R.O.M.I.S.E!"

"All right," says Bo. "Here's what you gotta promise. You gotta promise me that tonight, as soon as I give you my dog, that you will totally disappear! You won't even come close to me 'n your sister. You stay away from us all night. Agreed?"

"AGREED!"

In closin' out this true tale, it must be noted that back in the early 1960's, after spend'n three years with his Uncle Sam and shortly after his arrival back home in Tennessee, Curly's mom presented her ex-soldier boy with a box of forgotten old toys 'n keepsakes from his childhood. Some months later Curly was prowl'n through that box—and guess what?... Yep! There was *the dog*!

In 2019, Curly surprised his Sis as he handed her a small, gift-wrapped box and quipped, "Remember this?"... Sis had long forgotten her old wanta-be beau.... But she remembered... deLIGHTfully... the Dog!...

The End

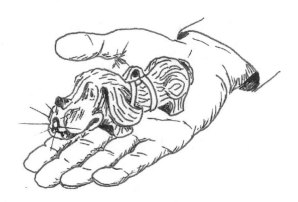

READER REFLECTION: Reader Friend, how often do you 'n your sibling (and/or family) enjoy rehash'n some of your favorite, delightful childhood "experiences"?

INSIGHT: Hmmmm…

28

THE 1942 CADILLAC

Revelation 1:8

*"I AM the ALPHA and the OMEGA,"
says the Lord God, "Who is, and
Who was, and Who is to come, the
ALMIGHTY." (NIV)*

Vehicle - Any device for carrying passengers, goods, or equipment. A medium through which something is... conveyed.

Automobile - A self-propelled land vehicle.

Car - An automobile.

An Unusual Story... About...

- A Lady... and Her Cadillac automobile
- A Boy/Young Man... who wanted the Lady's car
- The 1942 Deluxe Model Cadillac...

READER HEADS UP! Assume'n you have gotten to this point in read'n Bud's stories, you are now keenly aware that your personal participation 'n input thus far has been needed; but for this story it's a requirement... along with lots of imagination.

Ready?... Okay–Turn on your IMAGINATION ignition 'n start your engine... Here you go...

READER PARTICIPATION: As you begin this story, *please consider some of the various objects 'n animals, etc....* to which *people "assign" special and/or pet names.* Names which are used as nouns, pronouns, nicknames or "whatever"...

FOR EXAMPLE:

- *A (BIG) fish.* "*He* broke my line… *Big George* broke my line again."
- *A Squirrel/Rat/Groundhog.* "*He* ran into that big hole."
- *A Ship.* "*She* is a sleek, seaworthy vessel… *Lady Lucy* is *her* name."
- *A Car.* "My G'dad gave *her* to me… He called *her Betsy.*"

Before we get into this story here's what Google 2019 has to say about 1942 Cadillacs: December 7, 1941. Pearl Harbor. U.S.A. enters World War II. March 1942, General Motors ceases production of automobiles and joins the war effort via the mass production of airplane parts 'n transmissions for tanks. In the five months prior to the war, only 16,000 Cadillac automobiles were made… of which 25% were the *1941* models… resulting in the *rarity status* of 1942 Cadillacs. The '42 models were powered by the (then) famous V-8, 125 horsepower engines. One popular new feature was the ornate winged emblem that adorned the hood. Another new look was the rounded parking lights in the upper corners of the ample front grille.

So what? = In 1942, (when) consider'n the law of supply 'n demand being applied to the '42 Cadillacs, it's very apparent that Mr. Demand far exceeded Miss Supply— thus enhance'n the automobiles' *rarity status*!… set'n precedence of the excelerate'n high value that *21ˢᵗ century* Caddy enthusiasts place on the few survive'n vehicles.

... All of which...

Introduces this Story of a Teenage Boy's long flirtation with a *particular* 1942 Deluxe Model Cadillac.

It was not until 1957 that the boy saw the Cadillac for the first time. It was a case of FSF – First Sight Fascination. It was also an era when most high school guys were drool'n over:

#1) '55, '56, '57 Chevys.

#2) '55–6–7 Fords.

#3) Pontiacs of the same era.

However, this particular fella was most interested in *that* Cadillac. Not that he didn't admire the Chevys 'n Fords... he simply seemed to have his heart set on that '42 Caddy....

READERS HEADS UP! Older Readers will remember the sales pitch(es) that many used car salesmen utilized back in the 1950's, '60's, '70's:

"Garage kept–from day one..."

"Very low miles on this baby..."

"A real 'cream puff'…"
"This little beauty is a one-owner…"
And the real deal-clencher… "owned by a little old lady…
a schoolteacher… lived less than three miles from the
school… sat in her garage four months of the year."

Well folks, the automobile this young wanta-be auto
owner wished to get his hands on… to gain title of… was *not*
owned by a school teacher; however, the Cadillac definitely
was a one-owner… and really was owned by a Lady who
had brought her little beauty right off the showroom floor!

Look'n back, the Lady most likely had considered
part'n ways with her little '42 model at some point in the
future; but she sure wasn't in any hurry to do so. Nor was
the young fella in any position to make a final purchase
anytime in the aforementioned near future. Shucks! He
didn't even have a driver's license… but he did "own" a
legit *learner's permit*… and surely, his (personal) financial
situation would improve in the near future…. Chances of
make'n that Cadillac his own was look'n to be a possibility.
Hopefully, even more than a possibility!

Yet think'n 'bout it, he best not be dragg'n his feet…
not all of his buddies were focused on Chevys, Fords, 'n
Pontiacs. Garage kept, low mileage, one-owners weren't
seen every day and the Caddy this young wishful title
holder had his eye on would most certainly be described by
a car salesman as "a real looker".

READERS HEADS UP! With the original handbook/
owner's manual being unavailable, Readers must be
content to accept the hopeful "future owner's" personal
paraphrased description of his dream car.

*With an assist from above mentioned Google 2019. Her exterior could be described as follows:

Headlights - Large, perfectly round; very bright high 'n low beam features.

Grille - Ample in structure; perfectly designed to attractively accommodate the beautiful new parking lights.

Front Bumper - Design is an immediate attention getter... The two bumper guards being larger than those on most Chevy 'n Ford models.

Rear Bumper - Design is naturally somewhat larger than the *front bumper*–but is equally proportioned 'n equally attractive.

Apparently, at this point in the Story –the youngster had tired of all "formality" and simply describes his dream Cadillac in his own words: "She was a light tan color with a medium brown top... both of which compliments the beautiful high-chrome finished grille 'n bumpers. The white wall tires on her chrome wheels perfectly matched the grille 'n bumpers which made her one of the sharpest models around–Chevys, Fords... any of'm!"

The young man, intent on get'n acquainted with the Lady to whom his dream car belonged, soon discovered his dad–to his great surprise–was on "speak'n terms" with a couple of the Lady's family members.... Which eventually led to him get'n his first really close up look at the *Dream Car*!... and eventually, to his even greater delight, takin' her out on a test drive.... WOW! And Whoo-

Ray for driver's permits, because by the time he'd earned his *driver's license*, he'd also gained regular visit'n rights to the Lady's home....

Time seemed to literally fly by. Almost as fast as the Caddy owner's grow'n trust in the young man's ability to safely 'n properly care for her highly valued Cadillac... as did his belief that one day he would be the proud owner of that 1942 beauty.... Without a doubt, being behind her wheel, be it travel'n through town or countryside, it became his "most wanted" and favorite thing to do!

Not coincidently, by 1961, the young man had become well acquainted with the Lady and her family as well. Also, at this point in the story, world politics raised its ugly head. The Berlin Wall Crisis was in high gear... Uncle Sam was seek'n reinforcements... and so... the young man volunteered!

And... as soon as possible he wanted to take the Lady's Cadillac with'm.... It was ask'n a lot of the Lady! That car was the very *first one* she'd ever had. She really, really did not want to part ways with her prize. But you know what? She did!! Did not charge the young man a single penny... simply signed the title over to him and gave'm her blessings and sent him and *his* Cadillac on their way. He called that Caddy his "Baby Girl"....

Three years later the Soldier Boy returned home... *Him and his Cadillac*. Together, the Soldier and his Cadillac presented the Lady with two *little* Cadillacs.... The Lady called them her "Grandcaddies".

READER REFLECTION: It pays to be on good terms with one's mother-in-law!

INSIGHT: "…rejoice in the wife of your youth… May you ever be captivated by her love." Proverbs 5:18-19 (NLT)

My 1942 Cadillac… in 1961.

EPILOGUE
STORYTIME... THE END!

Epilogue - A short poem or speech spoken directly to an audience following the conclusion of a play. A short section at the end of a *literary work.

Well, Reader Friend, "Thank you!", for your participation in *Storytime*.... Together, we have managed to arrive at The End of our book of stories. And in keeping with the unorthodox style of this...uh... hmmm... *literary work, it will not surprise you that *Storytime*... ends where it probably should have started: Why write a book?... Obviously, there are numerous reasons books happen... And the reason for *Storytime*...?

Our title, *Storytime with Uncle Bud... Friends... Acquaintances... Strangers...*, is intended to be a few words of encouragement to the Friends, Acquaintances and Strangers along our life journey. Romans 12:8... Words and acts to simply encourage folks to live life one day at a time. Matthew 6:34... It's like us asking CHRIST to let us climb up in HIS shirt pocket and spend our day with HIM.... And for sure, we don't want to forget to let HIM be in charge! As that saintly lady Corrie Ten Boom so aptly stated, "Don't bother giving GOD instructions. Just show up for work." Also, as our friend and longtime missionary (to the Filipino peoples, 1996-2020) Kim Hughes-Cruse has often stated, "Tell people about the LORD... sometimes you may have to verbalize!"

In closing, Reader Friend, should *you* choose to make time to personally add *your* conclusion to this little book, we encourage you to do so! As you have noted while reading *Storytime...*, the cover page of each story includes a verse of Scripture that, when chronologically listed, reveal a brief synopsis of Genesis through Revelation.... The story of GOD's love and faithfulness to HIS people... conveying HIS instructions that enable HIS children (John1:12) to walk in harmony with our CREATOR!

Right now, you may very well be asking yourself, "Why write such a conclusion (to this book)?" Hmmm... good question. However, should you choose to do so, it could be as brief as rereading the verses previously mentioned and making your own list... yeah!... writing a few meaningful thoughts of your own walk and dependence upon the LORD... and of your own personal commitment to CHRIST! What a great conclusion. That's it. The End.

Give to the LORD the glory HE deserves!...
Psalms 96:8 (NLT)

Printed in the USA
CPSIA information can be obtained
at www.ICGtesting.com
LVHW010206130224
771717LV00006B/326

9 798890 412164